AMBIGUITY
OF SUFFERING

Nader R. Shabahangi, Ph.D.

A clarion call for those of us privileged to call ourselves awareness workers, psychologists, counselors, social workers, process workers and psychiatrists alike. Nader Shabahangi's words invite us into a challenging dialogue with Freud and Heidegger, two thinkers whose ideas forever changed our way of understanding the inner and outer world. Above all, Ambiguity of Suffering *alarms us to awaken from the prevailing narrative of positivism, and to enter a world rich with ambiguity, mystery, and meaning.*

— Troy Piwowarski, Psy.S., LLP, Licensed Psychotherapist

In this inspired re-contextualization of psychological epistemology, Dr. Shabahangi problematizes the very grounds upon which mechanistic influences of human behavior are predicated. Categorical diagnoses of the many forms of human suffering reflect an effort to eradicate pathological mental conditions, and yet, as Dr. Shabahangi demonstrates, the experience of making meaning as a human in the world compels suffering — just as the ambiguity of suffering, and all that accompanies its existential significance, nourishes the meaningfulness of being. From the orientation of Heidegerrian philosophy, Ambiguity *outlines historical and present-day mechanistic conceptualizations of the human experience, problematizes a reductive understanding of the human mind and spirit, and advocates for a more holistic conceptualization and treatment of the "problem" of psychopathology.*

— Stephanie Rothman, M.A., doctoral psychology student

AMBIGUITY
OF SUFFERING

Nader R. Shabahangi, Ph.D.

Second Edition, March 2015

Assistant Editors: Troy Piwowarski; Stephanie Rothman
Design and Layout: Will Clayton, Clayton Design
Published by: Elders Academy Press
624 Laguna Street, San Francisco, CA 94102 USA
415-861-3455 • pacificinstitute.org

Library of Congress Control Number: 0984709711
ISBN-13: 978-0-9847-0971-7

Printed in the United States of America

Elders Academy Press
A program of Pacific Institute

Contents

CHAPTER 3: Heidegger: From a Simple to a Complex Understanding of a Human Being 73

CHAPTER 4: Redefining Pathology: The Worldly Aspect of Suffering 109

This book is dedicated to all of us humans who take time to deeply know and experience other beings in this world — and allow them to be and flourish.

And to my mother, whose kindness and love for all that exists inspires me every day.

Acknowledgments

This work would not have been possible without the help and guidance of Professors Eckart Foerster and Rush Rehm, the resources and training provided by Stanford University, the many psychotherapy interns and students of Pacific Institute, and the elders and staff of AgeSong. Special thanks to my wife, Ladan, who encouraged and supported me throughout this long process.

Foreword

Ambiguity of Suffering appeared at a time in my life when I was struggling with an uncanny sense of dissociation from my own "worldliness." I had recently journeyed to California to take a sabbatical from my clinical psychology program in Michigan. I was uprooted from my familiar (and familial) contexts. *Being-in-the-world* felt foreign to me.

When Nader Shabahangi and I began working together, he mentioned a project that he had begun as a graduate student more than 20 years ago. The manuscript was essentially complete, but in need of a resounding conclusion. I read through the manuscript and was deeply struck; despite having rested on the shelf for over two decades, the message of the manuscript resonated with present-day dilemmas in psychology and psychiatry.

Together, Nader and I pondered what was needed to conclude the book; we decided that the final chapter needed to pull Heidegger's demanding language down from the ether and into the context of daily living. The goal was to paint broad, comprehensible strokes that illustrated a different attitude toward psychotherapeutics. Those broad strokes now constitute the Epilogue.

The fruits of our partnership expanded beyond *Ambiguity of Suffering*. As part of my research for the Epilogue in this book, I had the opportunity to sit down with experienced clinicians in the San Francisco Bay area who self-identify with the phenomenological perspective outlined in this book. I asked them how they applied a context-sensitive attitude to their work with clients. Ultimately, though these interviews were not utilized for the book directly, they helped me discover my own passionate curiosity about phenomenological approaches to therapy. Currently, I am embarking on a qualitative study to further explore this important perspective.

The legacy of this book — lived through Nader's teaching, his numerous elder-focused writings, his groundbreaking work in elder care, and ever rippling into new realms of possibility — is evidence of the vibrancy and passion that reside between its pages. This is not surprising, considering that the ideas put forth in this book are essentially a preface to the decades of Nader's service to elders. Just as Freud's *Project* became an underlying treatise for his later intellectual contributions to psychology, parallels abound between this writing and Nader's later contributions to existential and process-oriented psychology, as well as his revolutionary impact on elder care.

For example, as we read Nader's exposition of the Greek term *oikos*, which understands suffering as a community-felt phenomenon, we see a beautiful parallel in the AgeSong elder communities that Nader brought to life. These intentional elder communities are built upon the very foundation that suffering (as well as joy) is always already a community-felt event.

Nader is acknowledged in the field for his promotion of a new language for what is traditionally known as dementia and Alzheimer's disease. Beyond simply reframing these phenomena as experiences of "forgetfulness," this new language is infused with an appreciation of the utter mystery and depth of the forgetting experience, rather than focusing solely on what is tragic. This stance, too, is in these early pages.

Now, the next concentric ring of possibility unfolds as the words and ideas of this book find their way into your hands at this very moment. May you find (as I did) something in its contents that resonates with your own worldly context — with some aspect of you that was always already there, waiting for its unveiling.

— *Troy Piwowarski*

Prologue

This entire book reflects a switch from an understanding of the world that believes in a random universe to an attitude that believes in the purposefulness of life. In some ways the thoughts in this book are an exposition of the theme of living a life of questioning and curiosity. It is a belief that goes beyond the idea of "what you see is what you get." Rather than just collecting facts and information, we are trying to understand how and why it all came together. How did it all unfold? And what meaning do we make of it?

This book is my effort to re-introduce a love of philosophy to psychology. As Suzuki Roshi states, we're beginning to look again at the world from a place of not knowing rather than knowing — a world of possibility and probability, as opposed to fact and clarity.[1] Carlos Castaneda reminds us that one of our "enemies" of understanding is clarity: when you feel you have clarity, you stop questioning.[2] What amazing implications these ideas must have for those of us privileged to work with and help others.

It seems to me that the issue is not even with whether or not we live in a material or vitalistic universe — that question cannot be answered. My concern is with the belief that whatever story we might use to explain ourselves and our planet is no longer understood as a story, but considered to be reality itself. Scientists have stopped believing that their method is a mythology or a story. In so doing, science has made the foundational hubris of believing that it represents truth in itself. James Hillman was apt to point out that the biggest crime of humanity is the crime of literalism.[3]

In the field of psychology and its application of psychotherapy, it is unconventional to insist that the human being is complex and mysterious. I find this alarming. To understand a human being is literally to *stand under*. To me, this standing under means a way of saying that I stand in awe. As such, psychology, rather than being a scientific discipline, is understood as a container for all the many expressions of human consciousness — be that poetry, art, literature, religion, law, quantum physics, ad infinitum. Understood as such, the passion of psychology is to connect with *psyche*, the breath of life, the infinite expressions of the human spirit.

I cannot think of a deeper, richer, more beautiful and profound calling than to be an awareness worker — often called a psychotherapist — sitting or being in the room with another human being. Through their probing, awareness workers probe themselves. Through understanding their clients' stories, they write their own. Through being with their clients' suffering, they become aware of their own suffering. Through witnessing the depth of the other, they contact their own depth.

As such, suffering holds one of the deeper meanings of life: the ability to connect with your soul, your deep humanity. This connection with suffering pushes us to become ever more aware. Rather than trying to eliminate suffering, we can celebrate it as an opportunity to deepen who we are. In fact, throughout recorded history, humans have admired those who experienced deep suffering, those who have become transformed because of it and have persevered.

This book is also academic in nature. Using the term *academic* implies that this book will try to present *evidence*, which might slow the reading and appear tedious at times. I am trying not only to present arguments, but also to ground those arguments in evidence. This evidence is meant to corroborate my statements, much in the way modern scientists must show how they arrived at their research conclusions.

With the evidence presented, I would like to show convincingly why, with our experiences and existing viable alternatives, the 19th-century scientific-methodological paradigm continues to dominate the understanding of the human being in the fields of psychiatry and psychology as well as in most other helping professions. Specifically, I want to explore why this overly simplistic view of the human being is still held today. And why it attracts, along with similar positivistic therapeutics such as behaviorism, cognitive therapies, and neuro-psychology, so large a following.

The narrow view of the human being not only represents an unqualified return to positivism, but also a return to a mono-causal structured belief. This view is predicated on the idea that human problems, regardless of their complexity, can be reduced to one specific cause. I will argue that the *specific* problem does not belong to some material object but to a human being. Human beings are not isolated, atomistic beings, but instead find themselves always within larger systems — an insight on which the relatively young disciplines of ethnology, anthropology, and sociology are based. They are subject to a multitude of internal (genetic–physical) and external (socio-historico–politico-environmental) variables. The idea that one causal determinant can be found for a problem located within such a complex system belongs to an era confident in the *absolute* power of the sciences to solve the riddles of life. This power, however, has been challenged and reconsidered — by scientists, social scientists, humanists, and philosophers alike — especially over the course of this and the last century.

Why, when there is so much to see — as the last 100 years have clearly shown — do we confine our field of vision to a 19th century, Cartesian-based, positivistic, and scientific methodological paradigm? Why does this restrictive and limiting thinking dominate our present-day understanding of the human being in psychotherapeutics, in the way we try to help others and in the way we understand the reason and purpose of suffering?

As a way of answering these questions, I will outline a more appropriate conceptualization of the human being, one that permits a richer response to the basic question of what a person is and, therefore, how this image informs our understanding of the healing process. The appearance of biopsychiatry signals a return to the mono-causality of the mid-19th century neurological materialists who conceptualized any mental disorder as a disease of the brain. Given the historical significance of psychoanalysis and its influence on American psychiatry, my study will begin in Chapter 1 with a close reading of Freud. His *Project for a Scientific Psychology* (1895) reveals the degree to which he once was committed to the biophysical reductionism of human psychology. The mature Freud was able to move beyond this narrow approach to understanding the human being, even promoting the radical social implications of his theory. However, with the American focus on early, medical Freudian theory, psychiatry became especially vulnerable to its present-day medicalization.

Freud's early reductionist understanding of human psychology entered into his concept of the human being, as my second chapter will show. Here, I scrutinize Freud's interpretation of Sophocles' *Oedipus Tyrannus* (also known as *Oedipus Rex* and *Oedipus the King*) as it regards his discovery of the *Oedipus complex*, later termed the *cornerstone of psychoanalysis*. I show that the Oedipus complex reading of the Oedipus myth ignores many of the insights of classical Greek thought and, finally, is a narrow and limiting understanding of the Oedipus play. I conclude by exploring the way in which Freud's restricted understanding of Sophocles' play reflects his method (*meta-hodos* or *road after*) of interpretation.

Chapter 3 offers an extended critique of the limited understanding of the human delineated in Chapter 2. Using Heidegger's analytic of *Dasein*, the human being is conceptualized as *being-in-the-world*, emphasizing the inseparability of human beings from the world and from others. The concept of being-in-the-world offers a more complete understanding of the human situation because it refuses to see the human being as a material, isolated, discrete object. This complex conception does not allow for the exclusive treatment of human suffering (*pathos*) with biochemical, technique-oriented methods. Rather, I will show the essentiality of the *phenomenon of world* in which the human being *always already* lives with other beings-in-the-world.

Given the centrality in psychotherapeutics of ascertaining the determinants of mental illness and its appropriate treatment, the fourth chapter will look at issues concerning the concept of pathology. Nineteenth-century psychology borrowed the Cartesian-influenced biophysical understanding of pathology from the medical sciences and applied it to the understanding of mental distress. However, the continuing biomedical understanding of pathology disregards not only the phenomenon of world, but also the complexity and ambiguity of pathos (of suffering) as a mode of being-in-the-world, an omission evident in present-day psychotherapeutic diagnostics. Current ways of diagnosing, based on an exclusion of etiology, reveal the continued dominance of an attitude toward the human being that dismisses the importance of the worldly aspects in conceptualizing mental distress. These worldly aspects are composed not only socio-politico-environmental variables, but also of ethnic and cultural influences central to the individual.

The final chapter attempts to account for the *extra-therapeutic*, worldly factors that contribute to the neglect of a theory and approach in psychotherapeutics that would convey a more adequate description of human beings and their challenges in the early 21st century. Not only is psychotherapeutics a conceptually informed praxis; it is also an enterprise driven economically, politically, and institutionally. As such, it falls under the sway of a host of extra-therapeutic factors often at odds with a true therapeutic spirit — that is, providing compassionate and optimal care that meets the needs of the individual, worldly being. I will show that money and power have shaped, and continue to shape, present-day psychotherapeutic care. In light of these extra-therapeutic factors, this final chapter states the central question of my project most decisively: How does the positivist understanding of the human being continue to have a hold on therapeutic culture? What is so attractive about this paradigm that, in spite of its obvious fallacies and documented damages, it continues to dominate the theoretical framework of (especially) biopsychiatry and a host of psychoanalytically influenced psychotherapies?

These are not only academic questions. The present-day biopsychiatric treatment of mentally distressed individuals violates that which makes us essentially human. Countless patients who submit themselves to the will of mental health experts are being stripped of their subjective reality, of the potential to live the richness of their own possibilities. As I intend to show, the premises governing today's biopsychiatry reveal that psychiatry, along with much of psychology, has lost itself to a reductionist view of human beings. Ever since psychiatry returned a few decades ago to the reductionist understanding of mental distress prevalent in pre-Freudian days, it has given up the possibility of becoming a genuine helping profession. A society that condones — indeed, supports — this form of treatment misses what it means to be human, as it inadvertently pillages and plunders the human psyche.

To bridge this epistemic and social critique with its implications for present-day and particularly up-and-coming practitioners of psychotherapeutics and psychiatry, I conclude this final chapter by elucidating the direction from mono-causality to complexity and multideterminism. This is an attempt to map, so to speak, the territory that practitioners who heed the wisdom of the past century must traverse in their work with people in their psychotherapeutic and psychiatric practice. It is a map that lead all helpers and sufferers to a stance of deep humility in the face of the unfathomable nature of human beings, of our existence, of life and being itself.

CHAPTER I

Freud's Concept of the Human Being

When a theory has as many difficulties as psychoanalysis does, a useful way of trying to understand and order it is to inquire into the nature of the model of man that it involves.

— ROBERT HOLT

The Trap of the 19th Century Scientific Method

The beginning of compassionate treatment for the psychologically wounded, which was pioneered in the early 20th century by Sigmund Freud, is itself a fascinating chronicle. Its story is defined by intellectual curiosity and constraint, representing the conflicts of a man steeped in 19th century German neurobiology. As we shall see, at the outset of his career, Freud sought to uncover basic human truths through the scientific method that defined both the times and the man.

Freud's unique odyssey from scientist to clinician to revolution-ary philosopher of the human being and mystic of the spirit will launch our own odyssey into the unrivaled contribution of Freud to human interiority.

It is only fair to give the reader a warning about the difficulty of this journey. And it is impossible to appreciate the courage and radical-ism of Freud's ultimate theory of the human being without begin-ning where he did. The early Freud was captivated by the scien-tific method, where people and their sufferings were understood mechanically, as if they were machines that had overheated or simply needed an oil change. Much of the language that describes his early experiments is technical and confusing, and one might be tempted to search for an interpreter. There is the temptation to simply write him off as unbearably dull.

Undoubtedly, it is true that one's eyes can glaze over when reading some of Freud's early material. Nevertheless, I believe it is crucial to examine this weighty material if we are to fully appreciate the excesses of late-19th century scientific method. Why? For the unfor-tunate reason that this method, which Freud abandoned in his later years, continues to dominate psychiatry's — and now also psychol-ogy's — search for a "cure" to human suffering.

Now, you might ask, what is wrong with seeking to eliminate human misery and pain?

Good question. What I hope to illustrate for many of the millions of people whose children, parents, or friends are dependent on drugs to "correct" their psychological suffering is that *suffering itself holds the key to its own liberation*. Eliminate the distress, or simply mask it through drugs, and we are left with a culture numb to its own vitality. It is tragic that more than 100 years after Freud, the medical establishment, particularly in America, is still bound to a model that oversimplifies the depth and richness of human beings. Such an antiquated viewpoint lessens our dignity, complexity, and soul.

The Roots of Psychoanalysis

Psychoanalysis, as it was originally developed and as it is practiced, remains today an important method to help people in distress. From a practical point of view, psychoanalysis asks questions about how best to aid another person. This clinical perspective is one important aspect of what has driven the formulation of psychoanalytic theory. We should not forget the clinical motivation for theory formation in psychoanalysis, regardless of the many theoretical, sociological, and even philosophical uses for which psychoanalysis has since been appropriated. It is important to remember that even Freud himself, despite the profound emphasis he placed on theory building, would rather tolerate theoretical inconsistencies than consciously distort his clinical experiences.

Those clinical experiences, which began with the 19th century practice of hypnosis, would ultimately prove most vital to Freud's psychoanalytic theory. Freud was in his early twenties when he was first exposed to this clinical practice.[1] He knew that Joseph Breuer, 15 years his senior and a pivotal figure in Freud's life, had used hypnotism as an effective form of treatment for a wide range of maladies that were then exceedingly hard to define.

Let us look first at a psychic complaint common to 19th century clinical practice and its folklore: *hysteria*. The symptoms of hysteria were vague and diffuse and attributable, with few exceptions, almost exclusively to women. In ancient Greece, its classical root was as a physical malady of women who physicians believed suffered from, literally, a *wandering womb*. It was believed that a woman's womb separated from her pelvic region and was set adrift to wander the whole of her body like a ghost. During this curious travel, the woman was afflicted with all types of bizarre symptoms. She would suffer from headaches and fainting spells or from inexplicable numbness.[2]

Although the "hard" scientists of the 19th century had abandoned the idea of a womb wandering the body, they were determined that hysteria was a disorder that required correction. In some circles, hypnosis was gaining ground as the treatment method of choice. *Dementia praecox,* or "madness," understood today as *psychosis,* was, in Breuer's school of 19th century Germany, also believed amenable to treatment by hypnosis. However, the German scientific establishment, mired in its blind certainty of quantifiable neurobiology, was suspicious of what many considered the cultish aspect of hypnotism, with its apparent lack of scientific rigor. Theodor Meynert, then the most vocal and respected advocate of the take-no-prisoners German scientific establishment, demanded proof of the effectiveness of hypnosis, one consistent with the then-dominant scientific method. He boasted, "Cures prove nothing, they themselves call for proof."[3]

In 1885 and 1886, Freud spent most of his time in Paris, where he was influenced by the work of the French neuropathologist Jean-Martin Charcot. Upon his return to Vienna, Freud began to take hypnotism seriously, from a professional point of view.[4] In the spring of 1886, Freud documented his experiences at the Hospice de la Salpêtrière in Paris. He praises the work of Charcot in what is known as the *Paris Report.* Freud was particularly impressed by the manner in which Charcot diagnosed clinical material. This report provides early evidence for Freud's intellectual passion, evident in his struggle to understand the interplay between the psychic and the physiological, the mental and the anatomical, in the creation of human illness. Freud was astonished that Charcot, in his classification of diverse phenomena, could "sleep quite soundly without having arrived at a physiological explanation" of them.⁵ In *Studies Hysteria*, written two years after his work with Charcot, Freud explained the foundations of hysteria as "based wholly and entirely on physiological modifications of the nervous system."⁶ Toward the end of the article, however, a first mention is made of the Breuer method. Having outlined the advantages of hypnosis and how suggestions under hypnosis — concentrating on the particular symptom — can remove the disorder (the essence of Charcot's method), Freud stated that "it is even more effective if we adopt a method first practiced by *Joseph Breuer* in Vienna and lead the patient under hypnosis back to the psychical prehistory of the ailment and compel him to acknowledge the psychical occasion on which the disorder in question originated."⁷ However, Freud remained a cautious researcher, one still wedded to a biomedical notion of the human being. He concluded that "it cannot at present be decided with certainty how far psychical influence plays a part in certain other apparently physical treatments."⁸

Freud's Biological Inheritance

The 19th century witnessed the cultural worship of modern science. The philosopher Friedrich Nietzsche postulated that the scientific method won out over science itself. Nineteenth-century physics and mathematics, especially in the century's latter half, represented the standard by which other disciplines modeled themselves. These other disciplines included medicine in particular, as well as biology, anatomy, physiology, and neurology. To become a physician in the latter half of the 19th century required intense study of the life sciences, within the framework of a modern science determined by physics and mathematics. A full 150 years later, this academic program remains the dominant model in education, as we can see if we look at most academic institutions today.

Born in 1856, Freud came of age during a time when earlier romantic ideas of medicine gave way to this new neurobiological movement. Basic — and at times innovative — research in some of medicine's foundational disciplines complemented his medical education.[9] Robert Holt and Peter Amacher belonged to the circle of researchers who investigated the influence of Freud's physiological and neurobiological education, particularly as it influenced his ultimate formulation of psychological theory.[10] Holt claimed that "many — perhaps most — of the obscurities, fallacies and internal contradictions of psychoanalytic theory are . . . derivatives of its neurological inheritance."[11]

Amacher, who traced Freud's theoretical indebtedness to neurology from his early writings, agrees, stating that Freud, "in postulating a mechanism of hysteria and repression . . . fitted his clinical observations into the neurological scheme common to him and his teachers. His therapeutic method was very much of an innovation, but his description of the mechanisms involved in it rested on the concepts of orthodox neurology."[12]

Freud's Teachers

At this point it is essential to ask, How did Freud's physiology and neurobiology professors conceive of the human being? What was the working model they sought to refine?

Ernst Brücke (1819–1892)

Ernst Brücke belonged to that group of scientists who showed a strong aversion to the then-prominent doctrine of *vitalism*. Simply put, vitalism was the belief in a vital life energy, which some also called the soul or *élan vital*, that moved in and through human beings.

Brücke was not alone in his belief that all human phenomena could be reduced to physical-chemical forces. He was joined in the 1840s by fellow students who would eventually become prominent scientists in their own right, such as du Bois-Reymond, Carl Ludwig, and Hermann Helmholtz. The well-known letter of du Bois-Reymond to his comrade Ludwig best expresses this belief:

> *Brücke and I pledged a solemn oath to put into effect this truth: No other forces than the common physical-chemical ones are active within an organism. In those cases which cannot at the time be explained by these forces, one has either to find the specific way or form of their action by means of the physical mathematical method, or to assume new forces equal in dignity to the physical-chemical forces inherent in matter, reducible to the force of attraction and repulsion.*[13]

Such a dogmatic theoretical construct left no room for dissent or even basic curiosity. Unfortunately, many of today's hard-core scientists perpetuate this belief.

Under the tutelage of his teacher Müller, Brücke came to believe that the organism (or the person) was based entirely on physical reflexes. This passive reflex model reduced all functions of the nervous system to physical reflexes *exclusively*. This kind of model did not permit an entity such as *mind*, because it would constitute a force independent of the physical-chemical, or *legitimate*, reflexes.

Theodor Meynert (1833–1892)

The neuroanatomist Theodor Meynert, who led a psychiatric clinic, was a highly regarded researcher in his field. Freud studied with Meynert for five months and was deeply impressed with his work. Freud continued to conduct experiments in his laboratory for some years thereafter.[14] Meynert focused his research on the correlation between the anatomical structure of the brain and the degree of an individual's mental functioning. This effort concentrated principally on understanding the workings of the nervous system: that is, the transmission of *excitation* (information) along nerve pathways. According to Meynert, the association of sense perceptions made up human intelligence. This explained why Meynert confined intelligence exclusively to the forebrain.

Association psychology conceptualized mind as a "passive spectator to the reception and combination of sense perceptions."[15] In this model, the individual gained knowledge of the external world through the imprinting of sense data and their subsequent combination and associations in the cortex. Meynert perceived the ego (*Ich* in German or, simply and elegantly, *I* in English) to be an assembly of strong ideas that control cortical functioning. Problems with the cortex due to fatigue or strain caused dysfunctions of the ego. Concepts such as *will* or *reason* that could imply nonphysiologically based behavior were contrary to this passive reception model. This also held true for inborn or inherited *instincts*. That instincts were inherited was a point argued especially by Darwin throughout his writings.

Meynert's strictly physiological model of human behavior and action had a psychophysical parallel, in which physical events "paralleled" mental events and vice versa. His medical treatment, however, conformed to the established tradition of seeking only physical remedies for various forms of disorder. Here Freud took a markedly different path. He had already begun the treatment of similar disorders, some of which he regarded as having physical causes. Others, however, he believed had mental causes. For these ailments, Freud courageously began working with mental processes rather than with their physical manifestations. Thus began Freud's subtle, but crucial, deviation from his mentors.[16]

Sigmund Exner (1846–1926)

Sigmund Exner was another important teacher of Freud. He belonged to the same school of physiologists and neurologists as did Meynert and Brücke. When Brücke died, Exner became the new chair of physiology at the University of Vienna. This appointment attested to his professional standing within the scientific community. Exner clung to many of the beliefs of excitation transmission in the nervous system developed by Brücke and Meynert. He further refined their basic theories of excitation transfer, arguing for the existence of subcortical *emotion centers* from which sensations were channeled into the cortex, as well as to other organs. Let there be no doubt: this was an original and potentially controversial idea.

In this model, centers of pain and pleasure allowed organs to transmit their excitation, signaling either pain in the absence of food and drink, or pleasure when these essential needs were met. These emotion centers became important for Exner in his description of the concept of *instinct*. As with Meynert, established cortical pathways basically constituted the ego. Thus, for Exner, instincts were aroused by pathways; the association of ideas with an emotion center created these pathways.[17]

Exner sought to explain why a certain idea or memory could simultaneously produce a strong emotional reaction. He did so by proposing that the transfer of excitation occurred in both directions. Excitation was not only a phenomenon that occurred from the organs via the emotion center to the cortex. It was also, potentially, a transmittal from the cortex to the emotion center and the organs. Exner used this two-way transmittal system, in which the emotion centers took on a certain independence from the cortex, to account for the influence of bodily needs — in particular, the sex drive — on conscious processes: "One can note in an especially significant manner that the centers themselves — so to speak — are to a remarkable degree cut off from conscious processes, leading their own life."[18] Exner thus exploited the independence of the emotion centers from the cortex to explain the sex instinct.

The sex instinct, accordingly, was not inherited. Rather, Exner asserted that it formed itself through the stimulation of cortical pathways from either the cortex or the peripheral sense organs. Within his physiological model, Exner also tried to understand heterosexual and homosexual love, with cortical paths forming the basis of one's sexual orientation. Through outside influences, these pathways associated themselves with the idea of the same sex, rather than the opposite. In Exner's assumption of the important role of instincts, he would influence Freud's later theoretical emphasis on the very function of instincts to determine human behavior.

Physiological Model Under the Influence of Jean Charcot and Joseph Breuer

As we have already discovered, Freud's contact with Charcot and hypnosis techniques led him to question traditional treatments based solely on physical remedies. Still, Freud remained convinced of the validity of the orthodox physiological model for the explanation of behavior.[19]

Freud's numerous publications on this subject, even after his experiences with Charcot and his own use of hypnosis, provide compelling evidence of his continuing ties to scientific orthodoxy.[20] Summarizing his study on *aphasia* (1891), Freud commented that he "endeavored to show that the cause of this important difference between periphero-spinal and cerebral paralyses is to be looked for in the structure of the nervous system." He continued to explain the reason for this difference as based on the fact "that the reproduction of the periphery in the cortex is no longer a faithful reproduction point by point," that it is "no longer a true projection."[21]

The collaborative effort of Freud and Breuer in *Studies on Hysteria* (1895), a work devoted to an explanation of mental suffering, continued to be informed by a physiological model in its explanation of hysterical phenomena. In a theoretical discussion of hysteria, Breuer resorted repeatedly to neurobiological language, his initial promise "to make little mention of the brain and none of the molecules" notwithstanding.[22] It was Breuer who introduced Freud to the concept of *constancy*, namely, "that there exists in the organism a tendency to keep intracerebral excitation constant."[23] Hypothesizing an optimum state of intracerebral excitation, Breuer explained this optimal level in the language of association and reflex psychology:

At that level of excitation the brain is accessible to all external stimuli, the reflexes are facilitated, though only to the extent of normal reflex activity, and the store of ideas is capable of being aroused and open to association in the mutual relation between individual ideas which corresponds to a clear and reasonable state of mind. It is in this state that the organism is best prepared for work.[24]

What is striking about this passage is the extent to which even the most basic scientific observations are shrouded in a kind of linguistic mystique: the "facilitation" of reflexes means simply that they are activated or engaged. The specific metaphor of "facilitation" implies a certain formality, as if reflexes are being ushered to their ultimate purpose by the human brain, which, within this metaphorical domain, acts as a kind of mentor. This passage thus becomes a prototype of what might be called *personification*, as though strict neurobiological connection is insufficient to explain the complexities of human behavior.

Clearly, Freud had much work ahead of him before he could state, categorically and with a profoundly informed humanism, that optimal psychic functioning could be defined, as has now become basic to Freudian folklore, by the ability of the person "to love and work."[25]

Freud's *Project*:
A Step Toward a New, Scientific Psychology

The *Project for a Scientific Psychology* represented the most direct expression of Freud's grounding in the physiological and neurobiological beliefs of his teachers. It was written largely in 1895, shortly after he and Breuer completed the *Studies on Hysteria*.[26] Freud's correspondence with Fliess verified that the *Project* preoccupied Freud for more than eight months, from April 1895 to at least January 1896, the year of his 40th birthday. Ernest Jones, Freud's preeminent biographer, found it "a magnificent tour de force. Nowhere in Freud's published writings do we find such a brilliant example of his capacity for abstruse thought and sustained close reasoning."[27] The Fliess correspondence also shows the enthusiasm — as well as frustration — Freud felt during his research "to discover what form the theory of psychical functioning will take if a quantitative line of approach, a kind of economics of nervous force, is introduced into it."[28] This quantitative approach followed the precepts of the Helmholtz school: the idea that all human processes had their basis in neurobiological phenomena. As such, the quantitative approach assumed by Freud adheres to the basic terminology and concepts found in neurobiology.

Jones is correct when he describes, with misplaced enthusiasm, Freud's capacity for abstruse thought. The *Project*, even to well-educated 21st century minds, remains almost unintelligible.

It was in the *Project* where Freud attempted, for the first time, to establish a theoretical framework within which he could conceptualize the new scientific psychology. As such, the *Project* represented Freud's most thorough attempt to comprehend psychic processes from a neurobiological standpoint. Of equal importance, the *Project* represented Freud's last major theoretical work before the publication of *The Interpretation of Dreams*. The ideas and concepts first developed in the *Project* appeared throughout Freud's later writings, especially in his pre-war metapsychological writings, as well as in *The Ego and Id, Beyond the Pleasure Principle*, "Mystic Writing Pad," *Inhibitions, Symptoms and Anxiety*, and *An Outline of Psycho-Analysis*.

Understood within this larger evolutionary construct, the *Project* is best viewed as the original deposit for the overwhelming majority of Freud's later psychoanalytic discoveries.[29] It must be remembered that while today we think of psychoanalysis as psychological, for Freud it was biological.

Of greatest importance, however, is the fact that the *Project* has received very little attention in Freudian scholarship. Although this may be attributable, in part, to its relative late discovery within Freudian archives, this neglect probably reveals a bias against Freud's biological heritage.[30] Freud himself seems to have had an ambivalent relationship to the *Project*; toward the end of his life, Freud "did his best to destroy [the manuscript] of *The Project*."[31] (It should be noted that, to date, Peter Strachey has provided the sole translation of the complete works of Freud into English — a translation which, as Bettelheim has pointed out, is both misleading in its scientific language and in its exposition of Freud's theory.)

The *Project* has acquired a unique position in the history and theory of psychoanalysis, crystallizing the dominant beliefs and schools of thought of Freud's place and time. The *Project* represents the essential ideas of 19th century scientific thinking, while at the same time ushering in an era of human psychology that confronts the immense complexity of human motivation and behavior more common to the 20th century.

The *Project* is not a theoretical cul-de-sac that Freud abandoned once he saw its limitations, although this is precisely the view a majority of psychoanalysts and Freudian scholars suggest. What these practitioners deny is that these ideas form the foundation of psychoanalysis.[32] This historical whitewashing helps with the creation of what some historians have termed the *myth of the hero*. The myth of the hero disregards — consciously and unconsciously — theoretical shortcomings or inconsistencies of the heroic person by covering him or her with a mantle of infallibility. However, as Strachey emphasizes, "the Project, or rather its invisible ghost, haunts the whole series of Freud's theoretical writings to the very end."[33]

Peter Sulloway, who studied Freud's biological inheritance comprehensively, warns of two basic ways of misunderstanding the *Project*'s place in psychoanalytic history. One is to view it as Freud's last, desperate effort to cling to a neurologically based psychology, and the other would be to regard it as a dismally failed project that Freud subsequently abandoned.[34]

Sulloway reads the *Project* as a neurological document that contains physical explanations of most of Freud's important future psychoanalytic concepts. Sulloway's research shows that Freud never truly left the realm of neurology and biology to become a psychologist. He remained a biologist at heart for the duration of his lifetime. The biology of the *Project* is one that was strongly modeled on 19th century mechanics and physics. Moreover, Sulloway's research traces Freud's *crypto-biologism* throughout his psychoanalytic writings, a fact that Freud tried to mask later in his life. By crypto-biologism, Sulloway is referring to the neurobiological metaphor that informs, from beginning to end, Freudian psychoanalytic theory.[35]

Basic Idea of the *Project*: Quantitative and Mechanical Approaches to Human Mystery

Freud divided the *Project* into three parts. He began by outlining the theoretical basis of a neurophysiological understanding of human behavior, motivation, emotions, cognitive (and dream) processes, ego, and human consciousness. In the subsequent section, Freud used these insights to explain the psychopathology of hysteria, and he attempted an account of normal psychic processes in the last section.

Two principal opinions open the *Project*: The first thesis "is to furnish us with a psychology which shall be a natural science: its aim is to represent psychical processes as quantitatively determined states of specifiable material particles and so to make them plain and void of contradictions."[36] Freud states here that the existence of *excessively intense ideas* as witnessed in hysterics suggests "neuronal excitation as quantity in a state of flow."[37] Because of the principle of neuronal inertia (which Freud will later refer to as the *constancy principle*), neurons must shed off excessive quantity.[38] According to Freud, this explains the structural dichotomy between sensory and motor neurons, because motor neurons can release quantity taken on by the sensory neurons. Reflex movements form part of the effort to maintain discharge of built-up quantity in the neurons. In addition to external quantity, the nervous system must contend with endogenous quantities, which originate from "the cells of the body and give rise to the major needs: hunger, respiration, sexuality."[39] In contrast to external quantity, these major needs must be met by the external world and cannot simply be discharged.

The second theoretical opinion rests on "the knowledge of the neurons arrived at by recent histology."[40] The recent histology to which Freud refers entails the existence of neurons, which make contact via *contact-barriers* (synapses) that communicate through the *axis-cylinder* (axon). In linking his first thesis of the quantity-management of the nervous system with these recent discoveries in neurology, Freud speaks of a neuron as either being empty or *cathected* (connected) with an endogenous (innate) quantity.[41] This leads Freud to understand the single neuron as a "model of the whole nervous system with its dichotomy of structure, the *axis-cylinder* being the organ of discharge."[42]

Here we see Freud, one of the great prose stylists of any language in the 19th century *fin de siecle*, brought to his knees as he endeavors to explain, with clarity and conviction, a theory that has one foot firmly rooted in 19th century scientific mechanics and the other foot flirting, if you will, with a revolutionary understanding of the human being.

Memory, Freud contends, must have a choice. According to the work of the *Project*, Freud brings his theory of memory retention full circle. He argues for the independence of the psychic neuron by proposing multiple contact-barriers that are independent of each other. To further substantiate his hypothesis of the existence of two distinct groups of neurons, of the physical and psychic systems, Freud attempts to establish a biological perspective. The reader will notice here the excruciating inner conflict in which Freud is certainly mired. On the one hand, he understands that there is a valid distinction between the physical and the psychic, between body and mind. Nevertheless, he is compelled at this point in his career to explain the mind in terms of physical processes.

Why, we might ask, is any of this relevant to our 21st century lives? Precisely because the psychopharmaceutical industries of today are predicated upon mechanistic concepts of the human being (concepts ultimately abandoned by Freud). Specifically, the person is understood as a machine. This machine concept is used to market drugs to treat depression, anxiety, and restlessness — all things typical of human existence. Moreover, these very human traits are known by many to produce that which is exceptional in human endeavor. Can one imagine Mozart as anything but restless? Would van Gogh have become van Gogh without anxiety?

Freud's *Project* represents an attempt to approach human mystery quantitatively, or mathematically. Significant to the *Project's* quantitative approach to the human being was the concept of the experience of satisfaction. Though this concept related to pleasure/displeasure, it also yielded important differences. Peter Amacher stated that Freud's *experience of satisfaction* resembles Meynert's attempt at describing *individuality* or *ego* and remained close to the cortical pathways proposed by Exner. His schema provided important implications for instincts: "Most of the *Project* is a description of normal mental or nervous processes as complications of the experience of satisfaction."[43] For Freud, the experience of satisfaction had "the most radical results on the development of the individual's functions."[44]

How does Freud understand this concept of the experience of satisfaction? The phrase refers to the *total event* that encapsulates internal and external change in response to the accumulation of internal stimuli. The yield is what Freud calls *cathexis*. Here Freud maintains that "in the interior of the system there arises the impulsion which sustains all psychical activity. We know this power as the *will* — the derivative of the *instincts*."[45] Freud understands the expression of any kind of emotion (e.g., crying or screaming) as a quality of internal change, though classifying as extraneous change — "change from without" — any form of direct help from the outside, such as adult intervention on behalf of an infant or child.

Because infants use internal discharge (e.g., crying) to produce external change (e.g., the caregiver brings needed food), Freud regarded the interplay between these two modes of discharge as the basis for the development of communication.[46] Such an observation showed that he was well on his way to becoming a great champion of a new and richer vision of humanity. It was clear that this interchange between the internal and external — the foundation of human communication — had profound effects on human development.

Sadly, we are not yet out of the woods. Freud was still dependent on a language that was incapable of conveying these newly discovered complexities. Freud saw that this outdated language did more to obscure human behavior than to illuminate it.

The example from the *Project* that follows illustrates Freud at his most methodologically and linguistically imprisoned. The reductionistic language of modern 19th century science available to him simply does not have the capacity to express his discoveries.

Consciousness as the By-Product of Nervous System Processes

In the *Project*, Freud insisted that the experience of satisfaction resulted from the discharge of endogenous quantity through the total event. Internally and externally caused discharges promoted the cathexis of certain neurons with specific perceptions. These cathexes established facilitations between neurons and allowed for *reproductive remembering*. The basic law of association by *simultaneity* summarized this process:

> *The law of association by simultaneity operates in the case of pure psychic activity, of reproductive remembering, and . . . is the foundation of all links between the psychic neurons. We find that consciousness — that is, the quantitative cathexis of a psychic neurone . . . passes over to another . . . at some time having been simultaneously cathected from the physical (or from elsewhere). Thus a contact-barrier has been facilitated. . . . It follows in the terms of our theory that cathexis passes more easily from a neurone to a cathected neurone than to an uncathected one.*[47]

What Exactly Is He Saying?

I have included this turgid description of association by simultaneity to show the reader the extremes, the myopia even, of trying to understand the human being as just one more instrument of modern science. Perhaps nowhere in Freudian archives is the ambiguity of the doctor's struggle between neurobiology and clinical theory quite so striking. The result, I think we can agree, is the serious shortcoming of 19th century modern science to explain the radiance and complexity of the human being. In this passage Freud defaults to 19th century dogma: understanding consciousness as the by-product of nervous system processes. This description appears again in Freud's so-called strictly psychoanalytic writings, particularly in *The Interpretation of Dreams*. That this text should reappear shows how difficult it was for Freud to let go of the old reductionist paradigm of 19th century modern science. The *Project* revealed Freud's ambition "to bridge the gap between normal and pathological mental functioning, and so to reduce the general laws of mind to purely mechanical and physiological considerations."[48] But Freud also sought to give an explanation of repression within the physiological framework. This endeavor had a central role in Freud's preoccupation with, and ultimate authoring of the *Project*, and according to Sulloway, represented the "core of the riddle" that the *Project* had thus far posed to psychoanalytic scholarship. A letter to Fliess substantiated this point. Freud wrote to him that:

[t]his psychology [of the Project] *is really an incubus.
. . . All I was trying to do was explain defense, but I
found myself explaining something from the very heart
of nature. I found myself wrestling with the problems
of quality, sleep, memory — in short, the whole of
psychology.*[49]

The *Project* and *The Interpretation of Dreams*

Freud never completed the *Project*, and it was never published during his lifetime. In numerous letters to Fliess, he voiced frustration with his inability to achieve a purely mechanical explanation of pathological defense, or repression. The *Project's* style expresses the same dualistic, psychophysical spirit that Freud's teachers employed in their writings. This psychophysical parallelism made it relatively easy for Freud to move from a physical-mechanical position to psychological language and description. And Freud could do so *without* abandoning the conceptual structure of the physical-mechanical model.

It was not only in the *Project* that Freud's frustration (or struggle) with the limits of the mechanical explanation was evident. In *The Interpretation of Dreams*, Freud insisted that he wanted to "remain upon psychological ground." But even a cursory reading of this work shows the extent to which Freud resorted to physical-chemical biology in an effort to explain his psychology. Strachey observed that it "is no exaggeration to say that much of the seventh chapter of *The Interpretation of Dreams,* and, indeed, of Freud's later metapsychological studies, has only become fully intelligible since the publication of the *Project.*"[50] Freud himself noted in his paper on the "History of the Psycho-Analytic Movement" (1914) that he had essentially completed *The Interpretation of Dreams* as early as 1896, but did not write it down until 1899. This time frame placed *The Interpretation of Dreams* immediately after Freud's preoccupation with the *Project.*

This chronology is controversial. The prevalent view in the canon of psychoanalytic literature is that Freud's self-analysis gave rise to the discovery of formal psychoanalysis. This self-analysis was provoked by a psychological breakdown of some sort, suffered by Freud between 1897 and 1899. If so, how can we explain his straining for a new vision and new language so clearly evident already in 1896 at the writing of the *Project?* In fact, the seeds of psychoanalysis, already evident in 1896, explain why Freud states in *The Interpretation of Dreams* that his psychological hypotheses "must be left, as it were, in suspense, until they can be related to the findings of other enquiries which seek to approach the kernel of the same problem from another angle."[51] By "another angle," Freud is referring to the expected insights of neurobiological investigations that had eluded him in the *Project.*

Freud never broke with his assumption that neurophysiological mechanisms underlie the human being's various psychological states. This assumption hovered over Freud throughout his career. Many of the inherent contradictions and limitations of psychoanalysis relate to Freud's inability to relinquish a physical, or mechanical, model of the human psyche. Indeed, Freud's obsession with this model's legitimacy continued to occupy him in his ongoing struggle to formulate an adequate theoretical base for a psychoanalytic understanding of the human being: a model which was all-inclusive. Understandably, this struggle did not help Freud achieve methodological clarity in his later theories, which he wished to derive not from psychological ground, but from the mechanical model of his day.[52]

Victory of the Neurobiological Freud

Throughout his theoretical writings, Freud maintained the mechanistic concept of the human being outlined above. However, in his later works on society and culture he appeared to transcend his own theoretical bias, becoming more speculative than scientific. In his later years, he noted how happy he was to be able to finally speculate after having been bound to the so-called scientific methods of the 19th century.

We have concentrated on Freud's theoretical writings up to 1923 for the simple reason that the psychoanalytic writings that most influence current psychotherapeutic technique and theory are based on his work from 1895 to 1923. However, it is true that much of the psychoanalytic community discounts these post 1923 writings, regarding them as the product of an aging genius who lacked theoretical and scientific rigor. It is also true that in his later writings, Freud is not particularly interested in further developing the conceptual parameters of the human being. As a result, these later works do not contain such a clear image of the person.

As presented in Chapters 4 and 5, it was the medical, neurobiological Freud who became a sensation in the United States. Bruno Bettelheim, in his monograph on the mistranslation of Freud, noted that the founder of psychoanalysis was legitimated for an American audience through Strachey's hyper-scientific translation, one in concert with a medical model, which the American scientific community found comfortable. This made Freud acceptable and appealing within a psychiatric profession already steeped in the biomedical conceptualization of mental distress.

There was a quality of convenience regarding the ease with which the more fundamental and radical implications of Freudian theory were abandoned half a century later to return to the pre-Freudian approach to mental illness. In today's psychopharmaceutical climate, the early Freud, a gifted methodologist, has overpowered the mature Freud, genius visionary of a robust human psychology.

To me, this is a significant occurrence. This revisionism of Freud has important consequences for the way we understand and care for the human being today. In the next chapter we will focus on the cornerstone of psychoanalysis: the Oedipus complex. My intention is to show how Freud's theoretical presuppositions, governed by 19th century reductionistic and mechanistic models of the human being, determined his reading of Sophocles' *Oedipus*. As a case study, it illustrates the degree to which one's model of the human can dominate and powerfully affect the manner in which a person's distress is conceptualized and "treated."

Freud became so fixated by his mechanistic-biological model of the human being that he even saw it played out in a mythological drama, a stage play of antiquity. The absurdity of imposing such a view on a prescientific, premodern expression by Sophocles never occurred to him. Nor, for that matter, did it occur to Freud's psychoanalytic heirs.

In the following discussion I will show how Freud's neurobiological, mechanistic view influences his interpretation of the Oedipus play to such a degree that it actually distorts the very human elements that the play attempts to explicate. We will see that, in fact, it is Freud who gives Oedipus the complex.

Oedipus Without the Complex: Bringing Mythology into the Understanding of Human Beings

For hard to bear is misfortune. But good fortune harder.

— FRIEDRICH HÖLDERLIN

Sophocles' *Oedipus Tyrannus* has fascinated Western audiences and readers since it premiered in Athens more than 2,500 years ago. Here is drama in which the main character is made, again and again, to confront his personal history. Such a confrontation is far from idle entertainment. The journey to individual motivation, intent, and self-knowledge has consequences for the king, which are breathtakingly gruesome, even by contemporary standards. Oedipus, this solver of riddles and the daring individual willing to face virtually any challenge, was a figure who captivated the young Freud.

Fair enough. But why *this* story? Why this figure? And why was this story so compelling to a theorist of human experience?

It is important to remember that Freud did not set out to create controversy when he came across the play, *Oedipus the King*. To the contrary, we have seen that, through his embrace of the scientific method, Freud was in many ways a captive of a form of criticism, a way of seeing and knowing the world, which was both limiting and conventional. So it was this deeply conventional person who would ultimately risk everything on a story about a man who kills his father to marry his mother — and this in Vienna of the late 19th century. *Oedipus the King* somehow enabled Freud to better understand the immense psychic cost of unawareness. Through his desire to understand Oedipus' individual history, Freud "discovered" what he claimed to be a universal history of human psychic development, one which he was convinced every male held in common with the play's main character: "A single thought of universal value occurred to me: I have discovered love towards the mother and jealousy towards the father, also in my own case, and believe it now to be a universal experience of early childhood. . . . If that is the case, the gripping power of *Oedipus Rex* becomes intelligible."[1]

For Freud, the Oedipus myth is of prime importance for understanding human beings as forged, inherently, by psychosexual tensions. So seminal is the Oedipus myth in the development of psychoanalytic theory that Freud argued it was the cornerstone of psychoanalysis itself. But does Sophocles' tragedy conform itself, in fact, to a psychoanalytic reading that claims to have solved the essential riddle of this otherwise inscrutable text? Let us begin by examining those passages in *The Interpretation of Dreams* that best express Freud's theoretical explorations to a public largely unschooled in the interior drama of human development.

Freud approached the Oedipus text with remarkable insight for the late 19th century. His intellectual originality stands in sharp contrast to the conventional psychiatric norms of his time, which argued that psychoneurotics, or people suffering from neurotic symptoms, differed only in degree from so-called normal people. This position did away with the polarizing divisions between the normal and abnormal, the healthy and sick patients. For Freud, neurotics exhibit "on a magnified scale feelings of love and hatred to their parents which occur less obviously and less intensely in the minds of most children." Although Freud based his discovery on extensive clinical observation, he believed he had found a cru-cial proof for his insights through "a legend that has come down to us from classical antiquity."[2]

Of course, Freud was referring to the legend of King Oedipus, particularly as manifested in Sophocles' tragedy of the same name.

The play's historic and mesmerizing power was validation of his belief that children have strong, dynamic, and vacillating feelings of love and hatred toward their parents. In the enduring and *universal power* of the play, Freud found evidence for the *universal validity* of his psychoanalytic observation. After recounting the plot of Sophocles' dramatic explication of the myth, Freud summarized his own reading of the Oedipus myth: "The action of the play consists of nothing other than the process of revealing, with cunning delays and ever-mounting excitement — a process that can be likened to the work of psychoanalysis — that Oedipus himself is the murderer of Laïus, but further that he is the son of the murdered man and Jocasta."[3]

This revelation embodied for Freud the essence of the Oedipus play. He contrasted his position with what he believed was "a misconceived secondary revision of the material, which has sought to exploit it for theological purposes."[4] The theological interpretation understands the play as a tragedy of fate, a tragedy that contrasts divine with human will. According to Freud, the spectator learns that there exists no choice but submission to the commands of the gods. Such an understanding of the play leaves the viewer with a feeling of impotence, and therefore could not be the essential quality that has moved audiences over the centuries. Freud cites as evidence the fact that other plays addressing the issue of divine versus human will were lacking entirely in the dramatic pull of the Oedipus story: "Later tragedies of destiny have failed in their effect." Freud, crucially, turned to the question of why the |Oedipus play could continue to hold modern audiences in such thrall: "The explanation can only be that its effect does not lie in the contrast between destiny and human will, but is to be looked for in the particular nature of the material on which that contrast is exemplified."[5] For Freud, the uniqueness of the material resides in the ethical failure of a son who slays his father and marries his mother. Freud radically insisted that we, too, recognize the possibility of committing these deeds, and that "the oracle laid the same curse upon us before our birth as upon him."[6] From this perspective Freud has moved from observations about a classical Greek drama to dogmatic claims about human existence and universal exigencies.

Toward the Oedipus Complex

We may say that such rigid interpretation is attributable to an original thinker caught up with his own ideas. But Freud is not alone in his interpretation of *Oedipus Rex*. In *Freud and Oedipus*,[7] by Freudian scholar Peter Rudnytsky, there is an insistence on the singular contribution of Freud's interpretation of Sophocles' *Oedipus Tyrannus* to human understanding. Freud's interpretation yielded the discovery of the universality of the Oedipus complex for psychoanalysis. However, it seems odd that in more than 400 pages of captivating research, Rudnytsky never questions — or challenges — the very notion of such a complex. By accepting the universality of the Oedipus complex as a given, Rudnytsky uses the Oedipus complex itself to argue for the validity of the complex. In so doing, he is arguing for the fundamental validity of Freudian thought.

What can possibly account for such circular reasoning from an otherwise seasoned scholar?

We find a possible clue to this puzzle in the appendix, where Rudnytsky discusses arguments in an attempt to dismantle the Oedipus complex. He denounces Deleuxe's and Guattari's *Anti-Oedipus* as incendiary rhetoric; he blasts Girard's *Violence and the Sacred* as, at times, absurd, dogmatic, and perverse; and he closely criticizes Goodhart's reading of *Oedipus the King*. Within the course of this adamant criticism, Rudnytsky suddenly appeals directly to the reader in an effort to explain — even apologize for — his critique of most Oedipus interpreters: "It may seem an ungrateful exercise to rebut Goodhart's reading of *Oedipus the King* in such detail. But it must be borne in mind how much is at stake in this dispute over Sophocles' drama — nothing less than 'Western Humanism at large,' and in particular the textual foundations of psychoanalysis."[8]

Rudnytsky has so privileged Freud's interpretation that all others are derided and barred from entering the discourse. What is it about this *humanism*, about psychoanalysis, that Rudnytsky wants so strongly to defend? Why does a Western humanism need to be protected from alternative understandings of humanity, from different interpretations of human relations? What is so precious about psychoanalysis that other therapeutic approaches, other models, constitute a danger to Freud's textual foundation? Heidegger may point us to a possible reply in his remark to the French philosopher Beaufret: "You ask: How do we return meaning to the word *humanism*? The question intends to retain the word *humanism*. I ask myself if that is necessary. Or is it still not obvious what disasters such titles create?"[9]

Using the example of Sophocles' *Oedipus Rex* and *Oedipus at Colonus* and their various interpretations by Freud and others, we will try to understand Heidegger's reluctance to retain the word "humanism." This reluctance, in turn, takes on central importance in understanding a concept of the human being that differs fundamentally from the one presented by psychoanalysis. At stake may well be humanity, but in a different sense than Rudnytsky and his followers suppose.

Unconscious Wishes as Our Fate

A son's *metaphorical* desire to kill his father and possess his mother expresses an innermost childhood wish. Because dreams, for Freud, represent a form of wish fulfillment, he finds further proof that in our dreams we share the destiny of Oedipus. Through the visceral landscape of the dream, we "direct our first sexual impulse towards our mother and our first hatred and murderous wish towards our father."[10] The Oedipus play strikes us as horrifying precisely because the forbidden within us is realized through the main character; our individual and collective repression, in the face of the Oedipus myth, becomes little more than sham. As the chorus of the play turns to us directly, we are confronted with this wish again, with our long forgotten desire:

> *Fix on Oedipus your eyes, who resolved the dark enigma, noblest champion and most wise. Like a star his envied fortune mounted beaming far and wide: Now he sinks in seas of anguish, whelmed beneath a raging tide.*[11]

Freud understood that these last lines spoken by the chorus are addressed to us all. These lines remind us of our cultivated ignorance regarding the deepest urges of childhood, particularly as they rebuke cherished morals and reassuring notions of civility. Jocasta, the coveted mother of Oedipus, attempts at one point to console the young king by telling him that many a man has dreamt about sleeping with his mother.

Surely we can admit to finding such maternal solace a bit odd. In fact, this pivotal scene is further evidence of Oedipus' hidden agenda. As Freud would insist, "It is clearly the key to the tragedy and the complement to the dream of the dreamer's father being dead."[12]

The myth of Oedipus, as it was transposed by Sophocles into dramatic tragedy, is the story of the "reaction of the imagination to these two typical dreams." This constitutes for us the essence of Freud's reading of the Oedipus drama. Through personal and revelatory identification with the forbidden wishes of Oedipus, Freud was able to validate his discovery of unconscious fantasy life and the role it plays in the mental health of an individual. Instead of the manifest act, or "the deed" itself, Freud shifts the emphasis of personal development to *unconscious* sexual fantasies modulated by aggressive impulses. The radicalism of this insight cannot be underestimated.

Around a decade later, he would call this phenomenon the *Oedipus complex.*[13]

Universalizing Oedipus

Freud insisted that the king's mythological and personal experience is a universal experience. It elevates individual tragedy to a common phenomenon: "It is not (the morality of the play) to which the auditor reacts but to the secret sense and content of the legend. He reacts as though by self-analysis he had recognized the Oedipus complex in himself and had unveiled the will of the gods and the oracle as exalted disguises of his own unconscious."[14]

Beyond universalizing the Oedipus myth, Freud took pains to comment critically on the tragedy: "It is surprising that Sophocles' tragedy does not call forth indignant remonstrance in its audience. . . . For at bottom it is an immoral play; it sets aside the individual's responsibility to social law, and displays divine forces ordaining the crime and rendering powerless the moral instincts of the human being which would guard him against the crime."[15] By characterizing the play as "immoral," he judges its contents. Therefore, Freud's approach to the Sophoclean tragedy consists of two basic elements: the elevation of the Oedipus myth to a universal phenomenon and the labeling of this phenomenon as the Oedipus complex.

Ever the scientist, Freud utilized the methods of reduction and categorization. These methods, deeply flawed though they may have been, were developed by modern science to understand a confus-

---

ing world, and were perhaps appropriate at the time. But Freud went beyond the convention of labeling. He used his interpretation not only to lend proof to clinical observations, but also to explain their causes or source: "There is no possible doubt that one of the most important sources of guilt which so often torments neurotic people is to be found in the Oedipus complex." Ten years later, this generalization would yield to a more comprehensive pronouncement: "the beginnings of religion, morals, society, and art converge in the Oedipus complex."[16]

It is important to address the valid criticism that has arisen in the century that has lapsed since Freud first introduced the Oedipus complex. Women, especially, have rightfully resented Freud's subsequent development of the notion of penis envy, which is the female analogue to the male Oedipus complex in which men want to dominate their fathers and possess, even sexually, their mothers. On the other hand, he posited, women merely hoped to attain the status enjoyed by men. Freud did not develop a parallel theory in which women want to dominate their mothers and possess their fathers.

In the historical and cultural context of the Victorian and early Edwardian ages, full human capacities were attributed to men only. The most any intelligent woman could hope for was to yearn to be complete in herself. On the surface, this sounds reasonable enough. But in Freud's culture, full humanity meant masculinity — a tightrope that women would have to tread with great caution if they were to retain their singular integrity as women. They were asked to do this at the same time as confessing secret urges that had to do with wanting, essentially, to be male (conceptualized as the *Electra complex*). The reasons for wanting to be male were self-evident: in Victorian and early Edwardian cultures, masculinity was the ticket to full citizenship in the creative and professional worlds. Freud may have looked at this reality pragmatically as he refined his theory of human nature. Locked within his cultural mores, it may have seemed the only way to help women achieve cultural equality.

Oedipus and the Father

Does Freud's reading of the Oedipus play capture the complexity of Sophocles' version of the Oedipus myth? Or does Freud's reading create the complexity? To answer this we must keep in mind the complexity of myths themselves. We should also question the assumptions Freud labored under in interpreting the play. To begin with, what (not who) does Freud consider to be a father? Pietro Pucci states that Freud's early interpretation of the Oedipus play "psychologizes the father and already presents him from the point of view of his law that prohibits incest: it immediately puts the child in the guilty role and the mother in a relationship of complicity."[17] Rather than a single father, however, the play presents a host of fathers: Polybus, the gentle and affectionate foster father who, in spite of his caring behavior, does not influence in any direct way the adopted son's fate; Laius, the biological father who conceived the son but also wanted to destroy his creation, suggesting an ambivalent relation between father and son; and Apollo, the metaphysical father, whose oracle lays down the law and etches the course of Oedipus' destiny. Teiresias — as seer, priest, and messenger — represents Apollo's earthly incarnation. These various real and imaginary father figures are supported by different narratives in the play. Oedipus' royal paternity rests on mythical narratives, his lineage originating with King Cadmus. Polybus protects his own narrative of origin and Apollo asserts his narrative of *telos* via the oracle and Teiresias. In turn, the narrative of Laius, Oedipus' biological father, is supported by the oracle and a motley cast of witnesses who come forward during the plot's unfolding. Pucci appears to be captivated by this multidimensionality when he states "that the text suggests a complex and unstable vision of the father figure and of its roles, far from the one-dimensional object of some popular psychoanalytic literature and from the unfocused one of many a literary critic."[18]

The complexity of the father figure, whether real or imaginary, also calls into question traditional interpretations of *Oedipus Rex*. This is the succeeding play authored by Sophocles that brings the myth full circle. According to traditional interpretation, we have the struggle between fate and chance, necessity and freedom. These polarized readings render father figures iconic and absolute, neglecting to question the father's essentially teleological function.

From Gods to Unconscious: Relocation of Fate

Freudian scholars have taken pains to point out that throughout the play, there is complicity between fate and chance.[19] The oracle's prediction of the fate of Jocasta's newborn son leads her to order his death, for example. However, chance has it that of the many shepherds who may have blindly executed Jocasta's order, it is only *this* shepherd who feels pity.

> *I pitied the little baby, master, hoped he'd take him*
> *off to his own country, far away, but he saved him for*
> *this, this fate.*[20]

The complicity of *telos* and *tuchê* is also part of language. The words refer to both chance and fate, to the intervention of a god, divine *tuchê* (akin to destiny), as well as to the merely accidental.[21] In *The Interpretation of Dreams,* Freud states that the Oedipus play is not a tragedy of destiny based on "the contrast between destiny and human will," but is rooted in something that lies within Oedipus himself: "There must be something which makes a voice within us ready to recognize the compelling force of destiny in Oedipus."[22] These statements minimize the interplay between human will and divine fate. Instead, they relocate destiny within Oedipus himself. Freud thus locates fate within the individual, unlike the play, which leaves the question of the interplay between internal and external forces unresolved. (As many scholars have pointed out, it may well be this lack of resolution in the play that has accounted for its undying popularity for more than two millennia.)

With this relocation of destiny from the divine to the psyche of a single individual, Freud initiated a drastic revision of personal history. From now on, fate is an unconscious structure modulated by the Oedipus complex. The force of unconscious desire *within* the individual replaces the powers of the gods. According to this logic, it is the personal unconscious, and not the gods, that assigns people their fates. Prior to Freud, it was commonly the rulers of the heavens — the gods — who were the cast members in the theater of the human mind.

De-Psychoanalyzing Oedipus:
The Question of Personal Responsibility

In *Myth and Tragedy in Ancient Greece,* Freudian scholar Jean Pierre Vernant assails the Freudian reading of *Oedipus Rex* as an interpretation where the "historical aspect of tragedy remains totally incomprehensible."[23] Vernant states that Freud's analysis of the play "had no influence on the work of Greek scholars. They have continued their research just as if Freud had not spoken." Vernant sees in Freud, the psychoanalyst, the main reason for scholarly disregard of Freud's interpretation of Sophocles' play. When Freud employs the reaction of a 19th century Viennese audience to exemplify how his (and our) contemporaries continue to resonate with the accursed Oedipus, Freud "historically unlocates" the play. This de-contextualization of Oedipus is the interpretive problem.

A more full-bodied, authentic interpretation of the Oedipus tragedy requires an understanding of its original historical context — of the *Zeitgeist* of the play. Only by linking the play to the particular society that created it, in establishing the frame within which "communication was established between the author and his ancient public," Vernant continues, is it possible to "tackle the question of psychological content and the reactions of the Athenian spectators to the drama and to understand what the tragic effect was for them."[24]

The rise of the tragic genre that occurred at the end of the sixth century B.C.E. represented, for scholars like Vernant, a more global Western response to a perceived erosion of moral and religious order. With this breakdown, individuals were free to confront the motivation for their actions. Such freedom came, as with all liberation, at a price. People could now question openly to what degree their own will was responsible for their deeds. This was profoundly different from simply blaming the gods and washing one's hands of personal responsibility.

Suddenly, basic law was reconfigured to better tackle the question of individual responsibility via the "back door" of intentionality. Did someone willfully commit a crime, or were there influences that exceeded the individual's control? The tension between individual freedom of action and the imposed will of the gods constitutes the essence of tragic consciousness: it constitutes a consciousness specific to Athens 2,500 years ago, one which would be indebted to fourth-century Aristotelian ethics. Aristotle believed that classical "tragic tension" gave way to a rational theory of action. The Theban plays of Sophocles are staged within the mind-set of a pre-rational Greek culture, a fact Freud did not consider. With this in mind, Vernant poses acute questions for a Freudian:

If tragedy draws its material from a type of dream that has universal significance, if the impact of tragedy depends upon stimulating an emotional complex that we all carry within us, then why was tragedy born in the Greek world at the turn of the fifth and sixth centuries [B.C.E.]? Why did other civilizations know nothing of tragedy? And why was the tragic steam so rapidly exhausted in Greece itself and its place taken by a philosophical type of thought that did away with the contradictions upon which tragedy constructed its dramatic universe, by accounting for them rationally?[25]

For Vernant, tragedy lies not in what terrible deed or crime Oedipus committed, but in his struggle to understand to what degree he is responsible, personally, for the choice of his actions. Therefore, the tragic consciousness embodies the assumption that divine and human actions oppose each other, yet remain inextricably bound together.[26]

The Greeks carefully distinguished between two different kinds of love. *Philos* referred to the love between family members where "[e]ach member of the family is an *alter ego*, a sort of double or multiplied self, for each of his relatives."[27] Opposed to *philos* stood *eros*, the loving desire for someone other, an other outside the familial bond. French psychoanalyst Didier Anzieu, who critiqued numerous Greek plays and myths in Freud's fashion, does not distinguish between *philos* and *eros*. He regards the relation between Oedipus' daughters and their father as an indication that they "dream of becoming his companion." If Anzieu implies that the daughters dream of a sexual union with their father — then, as Vernant puts it, "it is Anzieu who is dreaming." Vernant does not find any evidence in the Greek tragedies for the existence of incestuous longings between family members. Ismene's attachment to her father or Antigone's bond with her brother Polynices are not examples of a hidden *eros* but rather cases of overt *philos*.[28]

The Play and the Complex

Can one find any legitimate justification for a psychoanalytic interpretation of *Oedipus Rex*? Can the Oedipus play be adequately understood as the inexorable unfolding of an unconscious emotional complex that desires to kill one's father and wishes, concurrently, to take sexual possession of one's mother? I would say not.

Classic psychoanalytic theory insists that Oedipus was unconsciously drawn to kill his father and sleep with his mother. However, this interpretation is problematic if one pays close attention to the text itself. Nowhere does it state that Oedipus was aware of the fact that Merope and Polybus were not his real parents. On the contrary, Oedipus remains so convinced about their legitimacy that he does not return to them after he learns the terrifying pronouncement from the oracle. Several times in the play Oedipus exclaims that he is the child of the ruler of Corinth. How can the psychoanalytic interpretation claim that Oedipus takes willful possession of his mother after he has killed his rival-father, if he had no idea as to whom he killed and whom he married? Oedipus does not see his real mother until he returns to Thebes. It is upon his arrival in Thebes that his mother is given to him in honor for his heroic freeing of the city from the terror of the Sphinx; *not* Oedipus but the people of Thebes make his "incestuous" choice. The text provides no evidence that Oedipus and Jocasta lived in any way like mother and son. On the contrary, after the discovery of their relation to each other, Jocasta expresses her horror through hanging herself, and Oedipus blinds himself in unspeakable shame.

A psychoanalytic interpretation concerning Oedipus' relation to his father seems also without basis. As is true with the mother, the son had never before seen his father, and the play's dramatic narrative reveals only gradually that Oedipus had killed Laius many years previous, in a youthful fit. How could Oedipus have intentionally eliminated the rival for possession of his mother if he did not know the identity of this rival, what he looked like, or where he could be found?[29] However, one event might make for a credible argument that Oedipus had doubts concerning his genetic origins, in which he knew, perhaps, that Polybus and Merope were not his real parents. The scene occurs during a festive occasion at his Corinthian parents' home. He recounts to Jocasta: "Some man at a banquet who had drunk too much shouted out — he was far gone, mind you — that I am not my father's son." Psychoanalysts interpret this event as indicative of the fact that Oedipus already knew he was not in the company of his real parents. Vernant disputes this reading: "We believe, on the contrary, that Sophocles' reasons have nothing to do with depth psychology."[30] According to Vernant, Sophocles inserted this scene to satisfy the aesthetic and religious requirements of the play itself, because much of the dramatic tension lies precisely in the slow build-up of incriminating clues concerning Oedipus' deeds.

From a religious perspective, Sophocles must heed the power of the oracle: "In tragedy, the oracle is always enigmatic but never lies. It does not deceive man but allows him the opportunity to err."[31] Oedipus does not question the oracle's pronouncement and does not further investigate its meaning: "[I]t is Oedipus who is [in the] wrong not to bother about the god's silence and to interpret his words as if they provided the answer to the question of his origins."[32] Vernant thus insists that Sophocles gives the following psychological reasons for Oedipus' mistake: he is too self-confident in his judgment and he "wants to be the master."[33]

Much of the play is devoted to Oedipus' attitude, his hubris. This treatment of hubris is commonplace not only in Greek drama but in ancient Greek religious, social, and cultural contexts as well. The psychoanalytic hypothesis that Oedipus "actualizes" an innate desire for both sexual union with his mother and a decisive overcoming of his father contributes nothing to a meaningful understanding of the play. Rather, it "force[s] it into the framework set up by a pre-established interpretation."[34] This could well be a case of "If I hadn't believed it, I wouldn't have seen it!"

Rational Solutions to a Tragic Conflict

As Greek scholars have taken pains to note, myths represent what they call a "neutral fiction," which is not concerned with good and evil. They tell of parricide, incest, and matricide without imposing judgment. On the other hand, as Vidal-Naquet states, the poet transforms the myth into a tragic play and thereby demystifies it:

> [A] literary work is not a myth and cannot be reduced to its basic elements. The myth can only facilitate the reading of the work to the extent that it differs from it, to the extent that we know — but

often we do not — what the poet has added and
what he has discarded.[35]

The American philosopher Martha Nussbaum points out that some critics fault Aeschylean tragedy for being "logically inconsistent"; that is, it is "rather illogical (to our way of thinking)."[36] Nussbaum contends that these critics seem to base their arguments on the belief that "modern thought has progressed beyond these confusions."[37] She posits that Aeschylean tragedy presents a more enlightened understanding of tragic conflict than do most existing philosophical or theoretical postures, which are too often preoccupied with resolutions to the problem of practical conflict. Nussbaum argues that these theoretical "proofs" are less authentic solutions than they are either flawed and inadequate descriptions, "misdescriptions," rooted in the failure of adequate observation. "Aeschylus has indicated to us that the only thing remotely like a solution . . . is, in fact, to describe and see the conflict clearly and to acknowledge that there is no way out."[38]

Nussbaum's reading assails the idea that modern thought has progressed to a point where the tragic element has been rationalized away. By equating understanding with perception, she underlines instead the inadequacy of theoretical solutions to the tragic, describing them as misperceptions of what lies close at hand. This process objectifies the dilemma and creates what

Heidegger calls *Vorhandenes* (present-at-hand). That is to say that it places whatever we want to understand *at hand*.[39] This entails, as Heidegger makes clear, that we shatter the ossified context as well as the preeminent role history has hitherto played in what we wish to understand. The location of whatever we wish to understand "at hand" entails, as Heidegger points out, excising the phenomenon under question from its ossified context and particular history — without which we will fail to understand adequately *its* own truth or meaning. Just as Vernant outlined the importance of the historical context for understanding the complexity and ambiguity of Sophocles' *Oedipus*, so Heidegger points out the necessity of including the phenomenon of *world* in our understanding of the human being. It is precisely this de-worlding or de-contextualization of the individual that led Freud to remove Oedipus from the context in which he is more rightly understood.

Happiness Is Not a Matter of Control

The shift from Freud to Heidegger constitutes much more than a change of paradigm, from psychological to philosophical interpretation of the Oedipus legend. In fact, it does not represent a shift — or modulation — at all. It represents nothing less than a fundamental departure from the customary conceptualization of the sense and purpose of people and their lives. Such a departure appears most clearly expressed through the very last lines of Rilke's *Duino Elegies*:

> *And we, who always think about happiness as something that rises, are deeply disturbed if a happy thing falls.*[40]

The original German speaks of *Glückliches*, a word difficult to capture in translation. It implies luck and fortune, as well as happiness and success. *Glückliches* is an expression that perceives, describes, and interprets some event as positive. We consider fortune as an occurrence that belongs to an upward movement in life, something that brings us higher, permits us to rise above whatever we conceive as being less fortunate, less happy. And often we perceive of fortune or happiness as something to be achieved, to be actively pursued, as stated so eloquently in the Declaration of Independence.[41]

Yet "a happy thing falls." Within this elegant poetic trope, Rilke expresses a very different and alternative understanding of life.

Rather than a progressive forward movement that we must control and sustain to achieve a "happy thing," Rilke proposes the precise opposite: happiness might not be under our own individual control, and hence we are not a kind of "despot" of happiness who can be given the responsibility of evoking a "happy moment." When we recognize that happiness can also take the form or appearance of a *fall*, then we are shocked. This shock presents us with an existential quagmire, in which we begin to suspect that there are forces at work beyond our control, that our normal perception and understanding of the world has fooled us. And we may begin to appreciate Friedrich Hölderlin's subversive axiom: that good fortune is harder to bear than misfortune.

In our customary interpretation of fortune as something that rises, we fail to see that luck might also be something that does not *appear* — at first — as fortunate, felicitous, or positive at all. Only within a more expansive model of human life and earthly existence does fallen happiness begin to acquire its fortunate meaning. We might add here a paradoxical statement, namely that comedy equals tragedy plus time.

In Search of Meaning in Life:
Confronting Fate Through Suffering

To return to Oedipus, we can see the critical difference between two possible readings. The first reading interprets the play's unfolding plot merely as a sequence of disasters. The second understands, instead, these apparently bitter events as necessary components of the personal life of Oedipus. Understood from this latter perspective, psychologist Rollo May noted that scant attention has been paid by psychoanalytic literature to the continuation of the story of *Oedipus Rex*. The story of *Oedipus Rex* is followed by the third play of the trilogy, *Oedipus at Colonus*. May regards the neglect of psychoanalytic attention to this conclusion of the Oedipus story as "a consequence of the literalistic interpretation of the myth as having to do with sex and killing the father require[ing] that we stop when these are worked through, punishment meted, and the situation accepted as at the conclusion of *Oedipus Tyrannus*."[42]

In striking contrast to the traditional psychoanalytic perspective, May believes the major theme of the myth is the struggle, price, and yield of self-knowledge and its painstaking achievement. Sophocles' last play, *Oedipus at Colonus*, thus acquires central importance, for it is here that Oedipus comes to terms with his actions by understanding the complex interplay between what he must regard as his own responsibility and what he can delegate to outside forces, to gods such as Apollo. This liberating and responsible self-analysis mandates that Oedipus reject any prescriptive moral code or established ethics. Instead, he relies on his experience and insight as parameters for understanding, and gradually achieves a degree of acceptance of those behaviors that violated sacred (and normative) directives. Through this process, he *creates* a morality, and it is his own.[43]

The audience, participating in Oedipus' struggle, cannot remain aloof from the character on stage: "because of . . . the impossibility of legalistic blame, we are forced into an attitude of acceptance of the universal human situation and recognition of the participation of every one of us in man's inhumanity to man."[44] Oedipus' search for acceptance poignantly dramatizes the search for meaning and sense in his life. Understood in this way, *Oedipus at Colonus* is a drama that also, in the words of Rollo May, is a play concerned with the risks and benefits associated with grace and our urge to share it with others once it has been painstakingly achieved:

> *I come as someone sacred, someone filled with piety*
> *and power, bearing a great gift for all your people.*[45]

And:

> *I come with a gift for you my own shattered body . . .*
> *no feast for the eyes, but the gains it holds are greater*
> *than great beauty.*[46]

Oedipus has only a fallen happiness. From where do his gains — his sacredness, piety, and power — derive? What has he done to deserve such nobility, to be capable of bestowing such gifts? The play shows the pain that Oedipus has had to endure; it vividly dramatizes that he has "suffered terribly, wrongs on wrongs, no end."[47] "Bloodshed, incest, misery, all your mouth lets fly at me, I have suffered it all, and all against my will!"[48] Suffering redeems Oedipus. The gods themselves — or else "the dark world of the dead" — sent Oedipus a special escort so that "the lightless depths of Earth burst open in kindness to receive him."[49] As the messenger states, Oedipus' demise is not an ordinary death:

> That man went on his way not with trains of mourners,
> not with suffering or with sickness, no, if the death of
> any mortal ever was one, his departure was a marvel![50]

The man who committed such horrifying crimes experiences a death that is at once beautiful and fulfilled. What greater gift can the gods bestow upon a mortal than to let him depart from his life of suffering and struggle with honor and dignity? The play ends with the chorus of citizens who bore witness to Oedipus' struggle comforting his daughters:

> Come, my children, weep no more, raise the dirge no
> longer. All rests in the hands of a mighty power.[51]

Heidegger lifts these final lines to illustrate his unique understanding of the genuine intent of Sophocles. However, Heidegger's personal translation of Sophocles differs radically from the customary translation, such as Fagles's, above.

So radical is this difference that the English translator of Heidegger's *What Is Metaphysics* cannot accept Heidegger's personal translation of Sophocles. For Heidegger's personal translation, in stark contrast with the traditional version, presents an understanding of the human person which does not separate the human being from the world in which he or she lives. In translating these final lines, Heidegger seeks to condense his understanding of the entire play:

> *Cease now, never more lift up the lament; for these events contain at every point, carefully preserved, a decision of completion.*[52]

By stating that events already contain within themselves the decision of completion, Heidegger refers to the many situations Oedipus was forced to confront, and how those challenges were crucial to the formation of something larger: Oedipus' life. This is what Oedipus himself realizes toward the end of his life at Colonus, when he states that "old prophecies were stored in the depths of all my being, which Apollo has fulfilled for me at last."[53]

Content Results from Method

We try to follow the soul wherever it leads, trying to learn what the imagination is doing in its madness. By staying with the messy, the morbid, the fantastic, we do not abandon method itself . . . . Instead we adopt the method of the imagination. By following pathologizing onward we are attempting to discover precisely the methods and laws of the imaginal in distinction to the rational and the physical. Madness teaches the method.

— James Hillman[54]

Freud's excision of the historical circumstances that influenced Sophocles in his dramatization of *Oedipus Tyrannus* has had the effect of awkwardly forcing the mythos into a tidy, psychoanalytic frame. Freud's psychologizing of the mythos has also mythologized psychology. In a letter to Einstein in 1932, Freud revealed his astute understanding of the reciprocal relationship between science and mythology:

It may perhaps seem to you as though our theories are a kind of mythology and, not even an agreeable one. But does not every science come in the end to a kind of mythology like this? Cannot the same be said today of your own Physics? [55]

Though Freud impressed a mythological story with the stamp of a reductionist science, he rescued the psychological insight contained within mythology from psychology's neglect. Prior to Freud, mythic themes were not included in psychology's purview. This is not to say that science has not been affected by mythology. In fact, *science comes, in the end, to a kind of mythology.* Within only a few years (and another world war), Freud's observation would provide the basis for a similar pronouncement by two psychoanalytically influenced philosophers. They demonstrated that the absolute faith in rationality, as set forth in the program of the Enlightenment itself, constituted a mythology.

So the Enlightenment project turns into a mythology. With this insight, Theodor Adorno and Max Horkheimer summarize their responses to the horrors of World War II and to the dehumanizing march of technology with its attendant bureaucratization of the Western world. These dehumanizing processes made the underlying purposive nature of rationality horrifically clear to the authors. Without a clearly defined purpose — something to be achieved — this type of rationality ceases to be rational.

The point the authors want to make is that our standard definition of rationality, what we often refer to as logic, is not some neutral or objective process that leads to something hitherto unknown. Rather, rationality is driven by a goal. Because rationality is goal directed, it must have an end in mind, some purpose. That which has a purpose is not neutral. What is not neutral is governed by a vision or a belief. Hence, this shows that rationality is subjugated by a belief. Beliefs are, by definition, subjective. Ironically — and tragically, given the world wars — it was precisely "subjectivity" from which the Enlightenment project, with its emphasis on rationality, tried to separate itself.

Purposive rationality proceeds by technique, which provides a repeatedly proven set of instructions to the knowledge seeker. As such, technique offers a fixed pattern of responses to the problems that it scrutinizes. Its method remains the same, irrespective of the object of its scrutiny. Method overrides content.[56]

It does so in this way: method frequently overrides what we manipulate or use in everyday life. Driving a car, using tools, walking, at times even talking, take place methodically, without awareness of *the way* we engage in these activities. But whereas these activities do not necessarily suffer from our oblivion to the content we manipulate (i.e., the driver does not necessarily need to know the workings of the car to use it), the issue takes on a different perspective if the content is a human being, whose individuality, complexity, and — as I will show in the next chapter — *worldliness* do not allow for the application of a method that disregards these special human characteristics.

Oedipus also follows a method. His procedure demands answers to questions about his identity: "Analysis is oedipal in method: inquiry as interrogation, consciousness as seeing, dialogue to find out, self-discovery by recall of early life, oracular reading of dreams."[57] What essentializes "oedipal" is not the content of Oedipus' actions but the way in which *he* analyzes his discoveries. Freud describes the method of Oedipus as one resembling the method of psychoanalysis proper. "Oedipal," both for Oedipus and in psychoanalysis, constitutes the predilection for self-knowledge, for a consciousness that defines itself as the limit of self-awareness. Oedipus' relentless striving for insight parallels that of psychoanalysts.[58] They, too, search for insight and seek to discover missing psychological links to arrive at an interpretation that will release the symptom, stop the compulsion, cure the phobia, or reduce the hysteria. Mythologically, it is Apollo who best exemplifies this striving, one which constitutes, essentially, a poignantly hopeful quest for sudden epiphanies, for swift revelations. This apollonic quest for insight contributes, more often than not, to blind-sight: "We are so fascinated by what we see, we do not see our seeing: the objective content of the insight stands forth and we lose the subjective factor that makes this content visible in the first place."[59] The seer is unaware that her or his seeing affects the object seen.

However, it was not the search for self-knowledge that propelled Oedipus into motion and urged him to seek counsel from Delphi.

A very different concern burdened him: that of his city. Hillman points out that mythology tells the story of nymphs who guard Mount Cithaeron. They come down the mountain, especially during noontime, striking anyone with a physical or mental ailment who does not appease them with an offering left on the side of the road, or soothe them with some bread, milk, and honey. The fatal encounter between Oedipus and Laius occurs deep in the murk of the nymphs' territory. Overlooking the required offering, Oedipus ignores the demands of the environment. The nymphs, inextricably tied to *this* geographic place, cause the tragic death, and ultimately its tragic consequence: a mortal plague that settles over the city. This simple oversight of geographic/worldly demand had deadly results for one person, hideous and agonizing consequences for the other, and the wholesale death of citizens, animals, and crops. Not only anatomy but also, as Hillman suggests, geography is destiny.

Oedipus Tyrannus, ruler of the city of Thebes, is deeply troubled by the wholesale dying of his people and the destruction of the *polis*. He listens intently to the laments of the Thebans, acutely empathizing with their sorrow and suffering:

> *My spirit grieves for the city, for myself and all of you. I wasn't asleep, dreaming. You haven't wakened me — I have wept through the nights, you must know that, groping, laboring over many paths of thought.*[60]

Oedipus absorbs the pain of the city. He *is* the city — they are inseparable. Individuation, as Aristotle has it, cannot take place without the *polis.* Intriguing, indeed, appears the relationship between Oedipus the person and his geographic origins. Hillman points out that the messenger received the child Oedipus at Mount Cithaeron, at those fated crossroads where Oedipus will later kill his father.

Thus, knowing oneself encompasses knowing one's world. Therefore *know thyself* necessitates knowing where one lives. Oedipus the king, in his determined striving for self-knowledge, is *blind* to other forces that demand attention. He is obsessed with his *meta-hodos. Method* is derived from *hodos,* "road," and *meta,* which in this context refers to "the aim" or "the destination" of the road. As such, the word "method" implies an a priori knowledge of the destination. In other words, the traveler already knows his destination. The significance of this will be elaborated upon later, but suffice to say that method is not a neutral bumbling along but a goal-directed journey. In the case of Oedipus, it is his method that causes his ever-increasing mental anguish. It is his method that causes Oedipus' sickness, as it also causes the sickness of the city. Oedipus' subjects, the Thebans, also had a method. Their method was to demand a simple solution to an intricate problem. They wanted a clear answer from Apollo and from the seer:

The solutions to the problem of Thebes present the problem of Thebes . . . . They (the solutions) are diagnostic signs. The solutions imagined by a patient for his illness belong to the image of the illness . . . How the patient imagines remedy and what measures he is already pursuing show how the patient is constellated by his condition.[61]

Oedipus searches for the self, for truth, for the answer; he consults Apollo, he listens to the oracle. However, Oedipus can understand the oracle only literally. In this way he is truly his father's son. Laius also listened to the oracle and consequently sought to kill his son. As Hillman suggests, Laius could have understood the oracle differently. He could have heard it as an appeal to pay attention to his son: "Study his heart, grasp his ways, for he has the potential for your end. He is the one who can show you how your life ends, the ends of your life."[62] But Laius is blind to the subtle, deeper layers contained in the pronouncement. He chooses the most efficient and straightforward route, and his blindness kills him.

Oedipus' temperament, his method, shows the same impatience. He hears the oracle and takes immediate, heroic action. It hurts him to leave Corinth and those he loves; he obeys the oracle through literal understanding, and in this blindness kills his father. Dominated by the search for truth, Oedipus has no tolerance for ambiguity; he possesses no psychological sight.

Psychologically blind at the beginning of his journey, Oedipus is physically blind at the end. His inexorable quest for self-knowledge leads to a renewed blindness. Psychic blindness leads Oedipus to interpret the oracle literally. The drive for clarity and obtaining truth obsesses him; he questions, demands, and interrogates. He is a man possessed of short temper, belligerence, and violence. At no point does he question the seer's response to his demanding questions. His character resonates exquisitely with the very method he employs. It is only when Oedipus has become physically blind that his means of searching and questing change. The very temperament or method that demands immediate and simple solutions is in fact the cause of the problems that need the solutions.

By contrast, the older, wiser Oedipus at Colonus, no longer seeing with his eyes but "seeing" by touching, holding, embracing, and waiting, is a man characterized by a new way of proceeding. He no longer demandingly questions the seer Teiresias for knowledge and truth. The search for quick answers has given way to a slow and deliberate Oedipus, one meandering with the help of his daughters through unknown territory:

> *Closer, children, come to your father! Let me embrace*
> *you — I never thought I'd feel you, hold me again.*[63]

For Oedipus, *meta-hodos*, following the way whose destination is known, has changed into *hodos*, simply "The Way." What has changed is that he no longer dominates his relation to the world and to himself, no longer imposes his destination on the road. He no longer feels that he is the one who has to know and control the direction. As Hillman points out, *content results from method*[64] — different approaches to the same problem yield different understandings of the problem. With sightless Oedipus' new way of approaching life, he discovers a truth that extends beyond the realm of subjective insight:

> *But one word repays you for the labor of your lives —*
> *love, my children. You had love from me as from no*
> *other man alive.*[65]

Freud, ever the psychoanalyst, could not follow Oedipus to Colonus. Entangled within his own psychoanalytic *meta-hodos*, Freud stops at Oedipus' discovery of his past, content to witness the gain of self-awareness. Not even the question of "for what" — self-discovery for what end — is posed. Self-awareness for the sake of self-awareness, for the sake of blinding insight? Self-knowledge as an end in itself?

The primacy of the self implies that the world surrounding this self remains secondary; it serves only as a means to the self. This devalues the world as such. Understanding the world as a means implies a world separate from the self. It is this common understanding with which Heidegger takes issue, ultimately opposing it, categorically, with his revolutionary conception of the human being. We will now turn to this philosophical revolution.

CHAPTER 3

Heidegger: From a Simple to a Complex Understanding of a Human Being

> *Rather, just this problem arises: what is the kind of entity in which the world is constituted? That is the central problem of* Being and Time *— i.e., a fundamental ontology of Dasein. It is a matter of showing that the kind of being of human Dasein is totally different from that of all other entities, and that the kind of being, which it is, shelters right within it the possibility of transcendental constitution.*
>
> — MARTIN HEIDEGGER[1]

I Am as Essentially Different From *It Is*

In Freud's *Project* the human being was reduced to a biochemical machine. Even his mythological investigation, as shown earlier, did not fully change this narrow approach. Heidegger's conceptualization is fundamentally different.

In a letter to his teacher, Husserl, Heidegger points to the central problem of *Being and Time*, namely, to show that the human being is "totally different from that of all other entities."[2] Heidegger's project strives to undo the understanding of the human being as set forth by the natural sciences. Traceable to Galileo and Newton, the understanding of the natural sciences defines all of nature as the movement of matter in space and time.[3] In the last centuries the progressive dominance of the natural scientific view in many of the human sciences has helped forge a method of understanding human beings that differs little from the way other, nonhuman entities are approached and understood. However, as Heidegger shows in *Being and Time*, the human being, the *I am*, is essentially different from a nonhuman entity, from the *it is*.

To differentiate the traditional concept of the human being from the Heideggerian concept of the human being, Heidegger uses the word *Dasein*. This literally means "being there."[4] By using the word *Dasein* rather than "human being," Heidegger wants to assure that the traditional understanding of the human being — an understanding which has led to its objectification — is overturned. Heidegger wishes to rescue the human being by bringing human beings back to their intimate relationship with Being itself.

Heidegger's language often sounds strange to those unfamiliar with his work. He feels that much of the traditional language used in theoretical or philosophical discourse supports a concept of humans that deeply confines a more comprehensive understanding of the human being. The language to which Heidegger refers — a language that uses, for example, concepts such as *consciousness* or *subject* — has a tendency to objectify and reify, to word things in a fashion that makes things appear static rather than in flux. These concepts also foster the impression that human beings can be understood separate from their world. In contrast, Heidegger tries to avoid these traditional terms and language by using linguistic constructs that stay close to the actual phenomena themselves. This explains the many hyphenated words or compounds with which Heidegger attempts to show his new understanding of the human being as *being-in-the-world*.

Another note regarding Heidegger's unconventional language: as readers, we are steeped in the conventional jargon that separates human beings from the world in which they live. Heidegger is challenging his readers to lay aside and free their thinking from the confines of what has become a customary understanding. This liberation from the customary way of understanding often necessitates a struggle with the new and unfamiliar way of looking at ourselves being in the world.

Though challenging, this struggle with Heidegger's unconventional language presents readers with an opportunity to move away from a reductionist, modern scientific view to a larger worldview, a broader understanding of humans and the world they inhabit. The use of the word *Dasein* is an attempt to fill this new concept with a broader conception. He wants to start with a clean slate, so to speak.

Heidegger was fond of saying in his lectures that a person interested in learning quantum physics would not expect that he or she would fully comprehend the complexity of such a new way of thinking the first time around. Likewise, readers here are asked to be patient with themselves as they struggle with Heidegger's fundamental challenge to our traditional modes of understanding. In fact, your frustration, though perhaps uncomfortable, is evidence that you have begun to enter the very process that Heidegger proposes: the letting go of old, confining ways of thinking about the human being in favor of a new, broader, and more liberating understanding.

Heidegger begins his argument by pointing out that the human being "is ontically distinguished by the fact that, in its very Being, that Being is an issue for it."[5] With this statement Heidegger highlights the fact that the human being is the only being who *relates* to its own being. To show the human being's intimate relation to Being, he terms the human being who exists, that is, who has to be *there*, a *being-there*, in German, *Dasein*.[6] Referring to the human being as Dasein, Heidegger points out that human beings, as long as they exist, manifest ways of being *there*. While humans are there, they *are* and have *to be*. The

---

relation of the "I" to its "to be" is of foremost concern to Dasein. Note that we say "I *am* in the world" to denote our existence in the world; we do not say just "I in the world." This relation, this being in the world, brings forth the many ways we concern ourselves with our own being. In this concern about ourselves we express an experience fundamental to our existence, namely, that we have *to be*. However, as Heidegger says so often, we are always already in the world. This means that world is neither a place nor an attribute but is a constitutive part of being. World and self are inextricable. We are always being *in the world*. To be is to struggle and face our possibilities of being. In this *having* to be, we always project the possibilities that lie in the future and, in this way, move constantly ahead of ourselves — always in the process of becoming. The moment we are not becoming, we are not being.[7]

Being-in-the-World

Dasein's essence is *to be*. This states that *existence* constitutes Dasein's essence. While Dasein exists, it belongs to me; it is mine. This *mineness* makes possible for me to exist authentically or inauthentically as myself. The way Dasein exists Heidegger calls being-in-the-world. This concept of *being-in-the-world* crystallizes the most radical break with traditional models of understanding the human being. Being-the-world is Dasein's most fundamental characteristic: "Dasein can be in existence because its essential constitution is 'Being-in-the-world.'"[8] The concept of *world*, as I will show, does not refer to the sense of comprising all the things of nature or the community of human beings, but indicates *how* beings live in the world.[9] Descartes had insisted on the primacy of the thinking of the subject, thereby separating object from thinking subject. For Descartes, the world became an object for contemplation separate from the thinking subject. Heidegger considers Dasein foremost as a being who always exists within a world. Human existence needs a world in which to exist. There is no possibility of existence without a world.

Existence and world are inseparably linked. As such, existence *is* the *essence* of the human being. One cannot think of world and individual as independent from one another. Because of this interdependency between world and individual, Heidegger uses the concept of being-in-the-world to describe the human being. The concept of being-in-the-world wants to assure that Dasein is not thought of as separate from the world. Dasein *always already* finds itself within a world. Heidegger expresses this poignantly as follows: "So if one should want to identify the world in general with entities within-the-world, one would have to say that Dasein, too, is 'world.'"[10]

Just as human beings have changed over the many generations of their existence and also change throughout their lifetime, so the world they inhabit has changed and continues to change. For this reason Heidegger understands human beings and their world as grounded in historicity; human beings and world are historical entities. For Heidegger, human beings' ontological ground of existence consists of their temporality[11] and, by implication, their finitude. The finiteness of the temporal constitutes the (hidden) ground of the historicity of human beings.[12] This historicity — the finitude of human beings — influences the kind of questions people will ask about their being. As such, no fixed understanding or evaluation of human beings appears possible, for they and the world remain in continual flux. The *worldly givens* and circumstances as well as human attitudes, preferences, and thoughts change in time. All human knowledge and understanding is bound to history (i.e., time).

Circumstances, Possibilities, and Choices

Again, Dasein constitutes the entity, which in its very being poses that being as an issue. In other words, only a human being questions the nature of its own being. Because of its continual concern for its own being, Dasein remains fundamentally *open* to its own possibilities. This essential openness of Dasein points to its need to make choices within a world of constant flux and change. The world and time in which it lives circumscribe the choices as well as its own limits and potential. Heidegger describes "limits" as *thrownness* and "potential" as *possibilities*. With *thrownness*, Heidegger alludes to the fact that we are *thrown* into the circumstances of a given time and possess certain unchangeable characteristics: for example, to be born a Russian girl in Moscow in the late 20th century as the third child of an Estonian father and a Ukrainian mother. Our thrownness largely circumscribes our possibilities.[13] As such, "[in] thrownness is revealed that in each case Dasein, as my Dasein and this Dasein, is already in a definite world and alongside a definite range of entities within-the-world."[14] Within these parameters human beings project their possibilities into the future to actualize what they are from where they are.[15] In projection Dasein discloses, opens, or frees up its potentiality-for-Being. Because of the structural significance of thrownness and projection for Dasein, Heidegger refers to Dasein also as thrown projection.[16]

Heidegger employs the phenomenological method in the analysis of humans in their everyday manner. Foremost, this means that he wants to understand the way human beings present themselves without resorting to "free-floating constructions and accidental findings" or "conceptions which only seem to have been demonstrated."[17]

Being-in-the-World: World, Who, and Being-In

Heidegger clarifies his concept of being-in-the-world by addressing the question of "What is world?" He states that this question is concerned with an understanding of the phenomenon of world and *worldliness*. He also asks about Dasein in its everydayness and is concerned with its fundamental characteristic of being-in.

As stated earlier, one of Dasein's fundamental characteristics is to exist, to be in the world. To follow Heidegger's explication of *world*, it is important to understand how Heidegger conceptualizes the phenomenon of *being-in*. A few introductory observations shall precede the more detailed analysis of being-in.[18]

To "be-in" does not imply its usual, spatial meaning, like some object that is in a box or container. The spatial sense of being *in* something indicates a categorical understanding of what *in* represents. Here, *in* points to the meaning of inclusion, of forming part of a collection among or with other entities. However, this inclusionary understanding of being in something does not set forth the primary way Dasein finds itself in-the-world. Rather, *being-in,* understood in the existential sense, refers to a being-familiar-with the world, a living or dwelling in the world.

The way we live in our home illustrates this point. Here the living-in does not so much refer to one's physical being in the home, but rather to one's connectedness to and presence in the home. The feeling of being at home arises through our relationship to the various meaningful objects that decorate it and make it useful, through other people sharing it, and through the meaning the home takes on as a place of rest, comfort, or work. One feels *at* home *in* one's home. Dasein's fundamental characteristic of being-in points to its basic involvement with other entities. Heidegger points out that being-in does not indicate some "property" Dasein possesses that it can choose to be with or not. Rather, on the basis of Dasein's fundamental relation to the world, Dasein can enter into relation with other entities. Heidegger clarifies this important aspect of Dasein with the example of touch. Only Dasein, with its concerned relationship to itself and to other entities in the world, can touch and be touched — understood metaphorically — by someone or something. A chair and wall may touch spatially, but cannot do so in the metaphoric sense:

> *If the chair could touch the wall, this would presuppose that the wall is the sort of thing "for" which a chair would be encounter-able. An entity present-at-hand within the world can be touched by another entity only if by its very nature the latter entity has Being-in as its own kind of Being — only if, with its Being-there [Dasein], something like world is already revealed to it, so that from out of that world another entity can manifest itself in touching, and thus become accessible in its Being present-at-hand.*[19]

In other words, only a being who already is in the world, in whom the world finds itself, is able to encounter this world. The chair, for example, is only spatially in the world and thus cannot encounter anything outside itself. The difference between Dasein and a chair that is only spatially in the world is that Dasein is already in relationship to what it encounters. Only Dasein, with its fundamental characteristic of being-in, can *experience* being touched.[20]

Heidegger's Versus Descartes' Understanding of the World

Heidegger's approach to understanding the concept of world differentiates between entities that appear merely present before us — what he terms *present-at-hand* — and those entities that seem useful to us. What seems useful to us we call equipment. Heidegger employs the term *ready-to-hand* to describe this equipment as things or entities that await our use.[21]

The differentiation between *present-at-hand* and *ready-to-hand* constitutes an important distinction. Humans concern themselves originally with things that mean something to them, things they can use. Only secondarily do they appear concerned with things that seem merely present. Heidegger stresses that we concern ourselves primarily with things that have meaning to us, because we use, know, or like them in some way.

Heidegger re-evaluates the Cartesian understanding of the world by emphasizing the distinction between *present-at-hand* and *ready-to-hand*. Descartes understood the things we encounter in the world through their physical properties alone. The laws of mathematics and physics define these physical properties. This definition pre-empts an understanding of human beings and other entities in the world in terms of what they mean to us or in the way they relate to us and affect our lives.

This Cartesian definition strips entities of their meanings. They are reduced to their basic material composition. Therefore, entities appear present-at-hand to us. However, this present-at-handness is a *deficient* mode of understanding the way we humans encounter entities in the world as meaningful to us. This deficient understanding of the world continues to dominate our perceptions today.

Heidegger strongly criticizes Descartes' understanding of the world as a *res extensa*, a thing to be manipulated. Descartes arrived at this understanding in his effort to find something indubitable: "I suppose therefore that all the things I see are false."[22] This supposition leads Descartes to the hypothesis that "body, figure, extension, movement and place are only fictions of [his] mind."[23] Descartes does begin to feel certainty about one element, namely that he thinks. Even if there should exist some powerful deceiver making him falsely believe that there appear things present to his senses, there could be no doubt that he thinks. Therefore, Descartes reasons that he is "precisely speaking, only a thing that thinks, that is to say, a mind, understanding, or reason."[24] To state that he is only a "thing that thinks" states that he is *not* "this assemblage of limbs called the human body," for "it is possible that all those images, and, in general, all the things one relates to the nature of the body, are nothing but dreams or chimera."[25] What does this all mean?

Descartes' position takes on the attitude that "certainly the idea I have of the human mind, in as much as it is a thinking thing, and not extended in length, breadth and depth, and does not participate in anything that pertains to the body, is incomparably more distinct than the idea of any corporeal object."[26] Having assured himself of the fact that "my essence consists in this alone, that I am a thinking thing,"[27] Descartes investigates the existence of material things around him as objects distinct and different from himself. He concludes that these material things "may exist in so far as they are considered as the object of geometrical proofs"[28] — that is, the laws of mathematics make them comprehensible. Mathematical insight constitutes Descartes' way of seeking an understanding of the essence, the Being of external or material beings. What *is* equals only what can be ascertained via mathematics.

Defining the essence of the world as materiality comprehensible through abstract mathematics alone, Descartes then must attach attributes to worldly materiality. In his example of the melted wax, Descartes understands characteristics such as color, hardness, and smell, as qualities "added on" to the object. But Heidegger asks, can the simple adding of these characteristics achieve an ontological entry to the essence of "entities within-the-world"? Does not the reconstruction of the skinned-off entity require always already "that we previously take a positive look at the phenomenon whose totality such a reconstruction is to restore?"[29] We can add only the reddish-brown color of mahogany with its particular hardness and smell to a chair because we had first already seen, felt, and smelled the chair in its entirety. We could not recognize the chair without these characteristics. Precisely those characteristics allow us to identify the chair by differentiating it from other chairs. Heidegger refers to this with his statement that presence-at-hand is a *derivative* phenomenon. That is, it has its origin in an observed prior wholeness Descartes would disassemble for observation and then attempt to reconstitute by adding on the very aspects that had been under observation. Think of this mode of understanding in terms of a house. The house is perceived and understood to be that which it is. With this understanding then the constituent parts of the house can be taken apart, viewed, and understood. But had the house not first been perceived as a whole, the display of such individual parts would make little sense and certainly not, in pieces, be called "a house." Heidegger makes clear that it is only because we have a priori knowledge of the characteristics of the whole that it is possible to go back and add the elements that constitute that whole.[30]

One cannot grasp the being of a substance by Descartes' idea of the *extensio*, nor can one know it by adding on its characteristics. Descartes' *thing-ontology* — the ontic understanding of beings — does not suffice for an understanding of the Being of beings. Rather, Descartes manifests but one possibility of the interpretation of the *extensio* as the fundamental construction of the world: "There is some phenomenal justification for regarding the extensio as a basic characteristic of the 'world,' even if by recourse to this neither the spatiality of the world nor that of entities we encounter in our environment (a spatiality which is proximally discovered) nor even that of Dasein itself, can be conceived ontologically."[31] In other words, by restricting himself to an analysis of the mental and physical things, Descartes *forgot* to understand the *phenomenon of world* itself. In seeing the details that make up the world, he is blind to the world itself. It is as though he ignores the idea that he needed the world itself as a phenomenon to begin with to derive the characteristics he seeks to understand.

What constitutes this *phenomenon of world* that Descartes presupposes in both his ontic description of entities within the world and in his ontological interpretation of the essence, that is, the Being of beings? In answering this question Heidegger clarifies first his understanding of the phenomenon of the *worldliness of world*. Worldliness as an ontological concept means the structure of a constitutive moment that a human being lives in the world. Having outlined the interdependency of human being and world, Heidegger regards world as fundamentally a *human* characteristic. Heidegger terms this characteristic the *worldliness* of the human being.[32]

In particular, Heidegger differentiates world as an ontic concept, which points to all things present in the world. However, as an ontological concept, world points to the Being of these "things" that are present in the world. World can also refer to wherein a factitious — that is, actual — human being, as such, lives; within this world Dasein can choose to live in both the public and private world. World conceptualized as worldliness contains the different worlds outlined above.

World Is Not Just Physical Matter Independent of Us

Heidegger understands world primarily as the "wherein a factitious human being as such lives." Prior attempts of understanding world did not take into account the phenomenon of worldliness and, as did

Descartes, overlooked the phenomenon itself: "This understanding has the character of a certain de-worlding of the world."[33]

Primarily, we encounter that to which we already relate. We cannot understand world as simply physical matter that exists independent of us. Therefore, the predominant natural scientific view of the world points to an incomplete understanding of how we dwell in the world.[34] We do not perceive entities we encounter as mathematical-physical properties the way Descartes defined them. Rather, they show themselves in their usefulness to us evidenced in questioning: *What for? For-the-sake-of-which?* Referring to the Greek *pragmata* as a term for things that one employs and cares for, Heidegger defines the *equipment* as that which we encounter as we care for ourselves and for others. Equipment never simply is or exists by itself but always finds itself within a larger equipment-context.

The structure of the Being of what is ready-to-hand as equipment is determined by references or assignments. In a peculiar and obvious manner, the "things" that are closest to us are "in themselves" [*An-sich*]; and they are encountered as "in themselves" in the concern that makes use of them without noticing them explicitly, the concern that can come up against something unusable.[35]

References or assignments give existence and meaning to equipment, and in this context, human beings fundamentally encounter and care for things. Therefore, Dasein as being-in-the-world "amounts to a non-thematic circumspective absorption in references or assignments constitutive for the readiness-to-hand of a totality of equipment. Any concern is already as it is, because of some familiarity with the world."[36] For example, an old chair we have inherited from a relative and a table under which we remember playing as a child show themselves not simply as a chair or a table to us. They mean something to us to the degree that we might feel saddened by their injury or loss. This indicates that these objects represent more to us than just some material item with which we can dispense easily or exchange for another item of the same category. These objects belong to a context, a frame of reference. Without such a frame of reference, without a prior familiarity with the world, human beings cannot encounter anything. In Heidegger's statement that "whenever we encounter anything, the world has already been previously discovered,"[37] he points to exactly this insight. In contrast, whatever lies merely present-at-hand before us does not convey any special meaning.

Because we are caught within the Cartesian paradigm that understands the world as independent of us, we continue to treat the world almost exclusively as a material world made of substances to which we are unrelated. In this approach to the world, we have forgotten that, besides the physical properties and dimensionality of the chair or table, there exists the life and history with which we humans have imbued table and chair; we have given them meaning. Heidegger points out the tendency to confuse the order of dependence: we think that we first encounter things present-at-hand and then add onto them our sentimental values or utility functions. As Heidegger shows, however, it is precisely the other way around. In fact, it could not be otherwise: we first have to disclose a world before we can encounter things as present-at-hand. In our analogy of the house, it is because we already know house that we can dissect it as an item at hand.

The "Who" of Dasein

The question of "who it is that Dasein is in its everydayness"[38] seems at first a rhetorical question. However, this question leads Heidegger to expose the deficiencies of the Cartesian understanding of the human being. Such an understanding posits the human being as an isolated subject existing in the world in the same manner as other, nonhuman entities. As Heidegger admits, the question of the who of Dasein seems ontically obvious. The who appears as the "I, the subject, the Self. The who maintains itself as something identical throughout changes in its experiences and ways of behavior, and which relates itself to this changing multiplicity in so doing."[39] According to Heidegger, moving from an ontic to an ontological understanding of the who of Dasein does not leave behind a definition that regards sub-stantiality as the "ontological clue for determining which entity is to provide the answer to the question of the who."[40] However, to define the who of Dasein as substantiality follows a present-at-hand under-standing of the human being. As shown, this understanding does not adequately describe the character of Dasein.

In asking the question of the who of Dasein, Heidegger places in doubt the given, ontically obvious answer to this question. He won-ders whether "[i]t could be that the *who* of Dasein just is *not* the 'I myself.'"[41] In the remarks that follow, Heidegger responds to an imag-inary interlocutor who represents the traditional approach of under-standing the human being. This approach not only presumes the "I" as something indubitably given but also finds it important to "bracket the world," including the world of other beings, to gain access to an understanding of the *who* of the human being.[42] Heidegger concedes that this approach may have merits of its own as a *formal phenom-enology of consciousness*. But he questions whether the "mere, formal, reflective awareness of the I of actions"[43] can disclose Dasein at all, and may even lead the existential analytic of facticial (matter of fact) Dasein astray: "What if the aforementioned approach, starting with the givenness of the I to Dasein itself, and with a rather patent self-interpretation of Dasein, should lead the existential analytic, as it were, into a *trap*?"[44]

To understand why Heidegger speaks here of the danger of being trapped by the traditional approach of understanding the human being leads one to understand his main objection to this tradition and, *sequitur*, the argument he holds against it. His principal objection refers to the traditional approach of understanding Dasein as present-at-hand or substantiality: "Even if one rejects the 'soul substance' and the Thinghood of consciousness, or denies that a person is an object, ontologically one is still positing something whose Being retains the meaning of present-at-hand, whether it does so explicitly or not. . . . Dasein is tacitly conceived in advance as something present-at-hand."[45] And he reminds again that "presence-at-hand is the kind of Being which belongs to entities whose character is not that of Dasein."[46]

Heidegger has clarified the character of Dasein as being-in-the-world. In so doing he has "shown that a bare subject without a world never 'is' proximally, nor is it ever given. And so in the end an isolated *I* without others is just as far from being proximally given."[47] Heidegger opposes what Descartes had postulated as absolute certainty, namely, the thinking subject that exists independent of its world. By opposing the certainty of the thinking subject, Heidegger also opposes the priority given to the mental world of the subject. For the certainty of the *cogito* became equated with the primacy of thinking and reflection over other modes of Being.[48] He stresses that the substance of Dasein does not constitute "spirit as the synthesis of mind and body; it is rather *existence*."[49] Understood as such, the *I* must be interpreted existentially, that is, in context.

It is remarkable that Dasein as being-in-the-world frees and encounters other Daseins who also possess the very same characteristic of being-in-the-world. As such, these other being-in-the-world entities called Dasein are always *there too, and there with it.* Thus, others — really and virtually — share the Dasein of the one.

Dasein and Others

Dasein is always *with* others. But one cannot understand these others as separate from Dasein but only as "those among whom one is too. . . . 'With' and 'too' are to be understood *existentially*, not categorically. By reason of this *with-like* Being-in-the-world, the world is always the one that I share with others. The world of Dasein is a *with-world* [Mitwelt]."[50] To clarify that he does not speak of others as not-me, Heidegger states that the phenomenological assertion "Dasein is essentially Being-with" is "an existential characteristic of Dasein even when factically no Other is present-at-hand or perceived."[51] Even a solitary human being exists essentially as being-with. This understanding turns on its head the conventional view of a single subject that can choose to be with other subjects. In Heidegger's understanding, Dasein's aloneness constitutes a *deficient* mode of being-with and not its primary way of Being.[52]

Understanding Dasein as *essentially* being-with-others points to important implications. The "immersion" of Dasein in-the-world in its being-with-Others makes it understandable why, as Heidegger has already indicated, it can be difficult for Dasein to be authentically itself, to be only itself. Rather, Dasein in its everydayness presents itself most often in the mode of what Heidegger calls *the they* or *the one*. This inauthenticity constitutes therefore a fundamental characteristic of Dasein, "a primordial phenomenon [that] belongs to Dasein's positive constitution."[53] As primordial phenomenon, the "Self of everyday Dasein is the *they self* [Manselbst], which we distinguish from the *authentic self* . . . As theyself, the particular Dasein has been *dispersed* into the *they,* and must first find itself."[54] Dasein partakes (and has no choice but to partake) in the norms and social practices of a given society. These norms and practices — the way we communicate both verbally and nonverbally, the way we eat, live, and work, what we find humorous or sad — all form part of the customs, standards, and practices in which we engage every day.

We rarely become aware of these norms and practices because we live so intimately with them. Yet, we live our daily lives mostly within these everyday practices. This leads Heidegger to state that seen "ontico-ontologically with an unprejudiced eye, [the they] reveals itself as the 'Realest subject' of every-dayness."[55] In some way we can speak here also of the phenomenon of why culture most often remains unnoticed: it is because we are so close to our social and cultural norms that they escape our awareness.

They-Self and Authentic Self

The they-self "disburdens" Dasein. It is distinct from Dasein's authentic self. Heidegger emphasizes that he does not value one self over another because both belong primordially to Dasein's existence. However, Heidegger does stress that the they-self has a tendency to prevent Dasein from becoming authentic. It does so by averaging and thwarting anything that is particular or extraordinary: "By publicness everything gets obscured and what has thus been covered up gets passed off as something familiar and accessible to everyone."[56] The danger for Dasein is to remain fallen (for it is primordially fallen) in the they-self so that its judgments, its way of living and being, simply present the ways set by the norms and practices of the public. To live in the public or they-self has the result that the "particular Dasein in its everydayness is disburdened by the 'they.'"[57] Disburdened by the *they*, Dasein not only has lost sight of the distinct difference between its authentic and they-self, but in so doing has also given up any responsibility for following its own particular life.

As already referred to above, Heidegger calls the being absolved in the they-self the state of *fallenness*. In this state, Dasein has given over its own self to the they-self. The state of fallenness is neither positive nor negative.[58] The they-self grounded in our connectedness to others forms the very basis for our sense of community. The they-self reveals who we are: "For the most part I myself am not the *who* of Dasein; the they-self is its 'who.'"[59] Again, the concern with respect to the they-self is that it can prevent Dasein from becoming its authentic self if Dasein remains there. The authentic self is not a subjective self or person. Rather, it refers, in the Kierkegaardian sense, to the "potential of possibilities" that each Dasein possesses as it lives in the world.[60]

Being-In as Such

Heidegger's prior discussion of being-in took place within the context of Dasein's way of knowing the world and in the analysis of the *who*, that is, the being-oneself of Dasein. The renewed focus on being-in serves a different purpose: "By considering [being-in] more penetratingly, . . . we shall not only get a new and surer phenomenological view of the structural totality of being-in-the-world, but shall also pave the way to grasping the primordial Being of Dasein itself, namely, care."[61]

Care is fundamental to Heidegger's understanding of Dasein. Without being cared for, an infant or child, for example, will cease to exist. As we go through life, if we do not care for ourselves — take, for instance, the basics of eating, drinking, and shelter — we risk our very existence. In a broader context, today we are recognizing also that if we do not care for each other and the world within which we live, we also place at risk our existence.

Heidegger begins his analysis of being-in by stressing the existentiality of Dasein. The purpose of outlining some of these important concepts of Heidegger's *analytic of Dasein* is not to enter into some philosophical analysis of his thinking or to give in any way a comprehensive account of his many and often difficult ideas and thoughts. Instead, I want to highlight characteristics that present examples showing how much Heidegger's different understanding of *world* influences the way he conceptualizes the human being. Further, these chosen characteristics influence most directly the theory and practice of therapeutics, as was shown earlier in the exposition of Freud's concept of the human being.

Heidegger lays open the existential constitution of the *there (Da)* of Dasein as mood and understanding. Mood presents one possibility for translating the German word *Stimmung* and refers to one's basic feeling at a given time.[62] *Mood* implies one's attunement to the world.[63] In everyday language, the individual's attunement to the world refers to one's *state of mind*,[64] how one feels or finds oneself in a given situation: "In a mood, Dasein is always brought before itself, and has always found itself, not in the sense of coming across itself by perceiving itself, but in the sense of finding itself in the mood that it has."[65]

Mood does not represent some psychological condition, something that comes and goes. Rather, mood belongs primordially to Dasein's existence. Dasein never exists without a mood and always lives in some way attuned to its world. This attunement affects whatever we do: "Any cognitive determining has its existential-ontological constitution in the mood of Being-in-the-world; but pointing this out is not to be confused with attempting to surrender science ontically to feeling."[66] By establishing mood as primordial, Heidegger counters the dominant position that feelings or affects represent side-phenomena or add-ons to some other basic disposition, like a Cartesian, scientific disposition, for example. The primordiality of mood places it beyond the categories of *psyche* and *physis*. Mood discloses Dasein's world. Mood is therefore the condition for knowledge itself because only Dasein's openness to or awareness of its world makes knowledge itself possible.[67]

Equi-primordial with mood is understanding, which belongs insepa-rably to mood. Because Dasein is the being concerned about its own Being, it is concerned about what it can be. What it can be *are* its own possibilities. This concern with its own being shows itself in Dasein's preoccupation with understanding its own possibilities. Understanding concerns itself with possibilities, and these possibili-ties relate to Dasein's being-there, or existence. The basic character of understanding relates to the actualization of Dasein's given pos-sibilities. This characteristic Heidegger calls *projection*. He calls it *projection* because understanding makes it possible that Dasein can project and understand its given possibilities.[68]

Understanding thus relates to Dasein's view of its world in which it *always already* finds itself. Understanding concerns itself with Dasein's existence and determines to what degree the world appears accessibly visible to Dasein. This visibility does not refer to actual see-ing but rather to the way Dasein is in the world.

Interpretation takes a central place within our attempt to understand. Interpretation derives from understanding. It does not constitute some disinterested, neutral, or objective activity where we "throw a 'signification' over some naked thing which is present-at-hand; but when something within-the-world is encountered as such, the thing in question already has an involvement which is disclosed in our understanding of the world, and this involvement is one which gets laid out by interpretation."[69] Heidegger names our involvement with what we interpret as "having, seeing and grasping in advance." This "fore-having, fore-sight, and fore-conception" explain why an interpretation can never be free from presuppositions. Instead, an interpretation always bases itself on assumptions. These assumptions are often difficult to discern exactly because of our involvement with what it is we are interpreting: "In every understanding of the world, existence is understood with it, and vice versa.... Any interpretation which is to contribute understanding, must already have understood what is to be interpreted."[70]

To understand something means to give meaning to the entity, the Being we have understood. Meaning thereby belongs to understanding and interpretation. As a characteristic of Dasein, it does not present "a property attaching to entities, lying 'behind' them, or floating somewhere as an 'intermediate domain.'"[71]

Humans make themselves intelligible through discourse. By talking, we communicate our understandings, our interpretations, and our meanings. Talk expresses itself existentially through language. The traditional view understands language as phonetic sounds to which meaning or significations attached themselves. This contrasts sharply with Heidegger's understanding of language. To him, language is already meaningful within a shared cultural domain or context: "To significations, words accrue. But word-Things do not get supplied with significations."[72] This means we start with a phenomenon in the world that we intuitively know exists and then find a word to describe it and make further accessible its reality. In contrast, the prevailing understanding of words and their meanings views this process the other way around. We have a word that we then fill with meaning. For example, this would mean that we first have the word *chair,* and then fill the word with the object on which human beings were sitting. The prevailing view looks at chair as an invention divorced from the fact that human beings have been sitting on them before they named them. Thus the chair is seen as separate from the human being and is presented to the human being with a false sense of discovery.

Similarly, Heidegger contests the concept of communication where individuals supposedly convey experiences or opinions "from the interior of one subject to the interior of another."[73] Rather, "Dasein-with *is* already essentially manifest in a co-mood and a co-understanding. In discour*se,* Being-with becomes 'explicitly' shared; that is to say, it is already."[74] Because Dasein exists — *stands out* with other existences — it dwells already "outside" with others when it communicates. To understand communication as something internal being externalized to be internalized by someone else again does not capture the way we communicate with each other. Hearing and being silent represent modes of discourse or speech: "[H]earing constitutes the primary and authentic way in which Dasein is open for its own most potentiality-for-Being. . . . Dasein hears, because it understands."[75] Heidegger emphasizes that we do not hear individual sounds, phonemes, or noises. We do not hear a "multiplicity of tone data" that we then piece together to make sense of what it is we heard. That we also can break up an utterance into individual sound units requires first an understanding of the utterance: "Only he who already understands can listen."[76]

In being silent, Dasein expresses another possibility of discourse. Silence does not mean that a person has nothing to say. Rather, only one who has something to say can have the ability to be silent: "In talking with one another, the person who keeps silent can 'make one understand' (that is, he can develop an understanding), and he can do so more authentically than the person who is never short of words."[77]

There Is No Subject Without the World

Heidegger takes as his starting point the existential given that Dasein exists in a world it has no choice but to inhabit, that "a bare subject without a world never 'is' proximally given."[78] The centrality of world for Heidegger's understanding of the human being becomes clear in his definition of Dasein as being-in-the-world. This explains why Heidegger, after first delimiting and outlining his project, begins to analyze Dasein by clarifying the phenomenon of world and worldliness. In giving priority to world, he turns around the conventional approach of understanding the human being. This conventional approach gives its first priority to an isolated subject that then must apprehend objects in the world. As we have seen, Descartes expressed this approach eloquently. In his search for the indubitable, he comes to the conclusion that he can only trust the fact that he is a thinking being: *cogito ergo sum*. To trust only the existence of the thinking being places in doubt the existence of the world. Descartes divorces the *ego* from its world and creates, in effect, a *worldless* thinking entity.

It is because of the presupposition of a *worldless* subject that the demand for a proof of the reality of the external world could at all arise. This demand bases itself on the desire to assure oneself of a world.[79] This leads Kant to find it scandalous that philosophy had not yet proved the existence of the external world. In contrast, Heidegger finds it scandalous that philosophy would demand such proof.[80]

Heidegger positions the human being in the world in the sense that *Dasein is its world*. To question the reality of an external world "does not make any sense" as long as one remembers that it is Dasein as being-in-the-world who asks the question, and who else does the questioning, remarks Heidegger rhetorically. This means that "world is disclosed *essentially along with* the Being of

Dasein,"[81] or phrased slightly differently, "[a]long with Dasein as Being-in-the-world, entities within-the-world have in each case already been disclosed."[82] Heidegger contrasts his position to that of Descartes:

> *If the "cogito sum" is to serve as the point of departure for the existential analytic of Dasein, then it needs to be turned around, and furthermore its content needs new ontologico-phenomenal confirmation. The "sum" is then asserted first, and indeed in the sense that "I-am-in-the-world". As such an entity, "I am" is in the possibility of Being toward various ways of comporting myself (cogitationes) as ways of Being alongside entities within-the-world. Descartes, on the contrary, says that cogitationes are present-at-hand, and that in these an ego is present-at-hand too as a worldless res cogitans.*[83]

That one can think of isolated, wordless subjects that "join together with a world" requires that "the primordial phenomenon of Being-in-the-world [is] shattered."[84] Heidegger links this shattering to an "overlooking" of the *phenomenon of world*. In this inauthentic way of being, Dasein no longer understands itself as a being in the world but as separate *from* the world.[85]

Being-in-the-World:
Not Divisible into Parts for Independent Study

This chapter has explained Heidegger's understanding of the human being as a being who *exists* foremost *in* a world. Human beings as beings-in-the-world *are essentially* their world. Through this essential link, humans possess a prior familiarity with this world, a familiarity that forms the very requirement and basis for an understanding of themselves and world. This implies that an understanding of oneself and other entities in the world is grounded in a reciprocal relationship, in a *hermeneutic circle*: world and self influence how this very world and self are understood at any given time. Heidegger regards this circular structure of understanding not as a liability, as does much of the philosophical tradition, but rather as an asset.[86]

This understanding contrasts sharply with the belief in a reality independent of the human being. There, the *real* or *truth* resides in an independent reality, a reality beholden through *pure perception*: "[It] has long been held that the way to grasp the Real is by that kind of knowing which is characterized by beholding [das anschauende Erkenne] . . . . Primordial and genuine truth lies in pure beholding. This thesis has remained the foundation of western philosophy ever since [Parmenides]."[87] *Pure beholding* manifests itself in a detached, theoretical perception of entities that de-contextualizes or de-worlds what it sees. The world-context, the frame of references or assignments, escapes us.

This then gives priority to a present-at-hand understanding of the human being.[88]

Let us return to a central point of my thesis, namely to the question, What indicators could provide assurance for the fact that the present-at-hand understanding does not allow for a comprehensive understanding of the person in need of help? Why should this understanding be augmented by the more complete conception of the human being as being-in-the-world?

In my understanding, the Heideggerian conception of Dasein as being-in-the-world represents a more comprehensive, humane, and 21st century understanding of the human being than does the prevalent Cartesian view. The being-in-the-world concept constitutes a more comprehensive model because of its ability to include the present dominant concept of the human being as well as acknowledging new insights such as those given by quantum physics. Rather than denying insights because they do not fit established theories, the new concept of the human being establishes humans as beings-in-the-world. To view human beings as independent from the world is inconsistent with the understanding we have achieved in this century about humans living in complex systems.

Because the concept of pathology — of what constitutes mental distress — lies at the core of modern psychiatry and psychology, I will focus in the next chapter on an understanding of the complexity of this concept. It is the understanding of an individual's pathology that, in theory, should guide the clinician's treatment approach or methodology. Understanding how present-day psychotherapeutics conceptualizes pathology will offer an insight into current mental health care. This investigation applies the insights gained through Heidegger's conceptualization of the human being to a worldly understanding of pathology.

CHAPTER 4

Redefining Pathology: The Worldly Aspect of Suffering

The soul can exist without its therapists but not without its afflictions.

— JAMES HILLMAN

The curious blending and duality in the emotions of the Dionysian revelers remind us — as medicines remind us of deadly poisons — of the phenomenon that pain begets joy.

— FRIEDRICH NIETZSCHE

The Right of Citizenship for Suffering

In the late 1970s, Italy liberated its hospitalized psychiatric patients by enacting a law that did not allow people to be held against their will. This led to most psychiatric patients leaving the various hospitals across the country. Melvin Konner tells about an exception to this freeing of psychiatric residents, which involved a group of patients at the psychiatric hospital Santa Maria della Pietà in Rome.[1]

Feeling that their patients would benefit more from caring assistance and guidance than from an independent, free life without supervision, the administration of Santa Maria della Pietà embarked on an unauthorized experiment. They kept a group of patients until 1988, at which time some of the hospital staff took residents on an outing from which they never returned.

Patients and staff moved to a house in the small lakeside town of Bracciano, where they worked together in an unorthodox treatment of so-called mental illness. After the first year, patient interviews indicated that residents felt more at peace in this small town, that the lake "kept your personality calm," that they enjoyed having more responsibility, and experienced a type of therapeutic relief at no longer having to depend on the hospital anymore. At a town meeting, the mayor, Dr. Sigillo, a physician, was "filled with joy" that renewed efforts were being made to help these patients. He remarked with pride that the mentally ill belonged to his community — that they were now legitimate citizens of a community.[2] Dr. Losavio of Santa Maria della Pietà expressed the profound and radical outcome of integrating the mentally ill within the community of Bracciano, of treating psychiatric patients among other, "normal" people:

> *I don't think that it's enough: to find a house, where you can put people outside the psychiatric hospital, because that house itself can become a small asylum. It is important that this reality has its real location in the*

village, the borough where the people live, and that the community acknowledges this situation, not any more as strange, alien, but a reality which belongs to that community. If these people are recognized as citizens of this village, the village itself is transformed, because it becomes conscious of a reality which belongs to it, not imposed from outside, but a suffering which, in one way or another, exists in the village.[3]

The suffering itself is given a right of citizenship, and this allows the house not to be separated, excluded, but to be part of this context of life.[4]

It is difficult to conceive of a more eloquent way of phrasing the leitmotif of this chapter, namely that *suffering itself is given a right of citizenship*. Over the last centuries, increasingly suffering has been denied this citizenship and has come to be understood as aberrant, devious, and sick. As discussed in Chapter 2, Freud understood the immense suffering of Oedipus as a *complex*, a failure to comprehend the past. Freud did not want to see to what end all this horrific suffering led Oedipus. He did not want to follow Oedipus to Colonus where he understood something about other dimensions; he understood that "[a]ll rests in the hands of a mighty power."[5] There Oedipus also realized his feelings for his daughters and learned more about love. Freud stops at the point where Oedipus begins another journey, where he slouches toward his grave and goes beyond his self, realizing that his shattered body "holds gifts greater than great beauty."[6]

This chapter will examine how a being-in-the-world understanding of human beings leads to a different conception of pathology, or suffering. As beings-in-the-world, people *are* their world, live *always already* with others. What I do in the world impacts world, self, and others as much as world impacts me, others, and itself. Suffering is a part of world, part of the human experience. By denying it citizenship, to our detriment, we deny part of a world that co-exists with us and belongs essentially to our constitution.

The Concept of Pathology:
From Suffering to Physiological Disturbance

Pathology originates from a composite of the two Greek words "pathos" and "logos." In its original meaning, pathos signifies suffering, enduring, feeling, and emotion.[7] Logos, in this context, has come to mean the *study of* some subject or topic. Until the last century, the English language used, though rarely, pathos as a term to refer to the condition of suffering itself. It continues to be used in the arts to refer to "the exciting of feelings of pity or sadness" and the "power of stirring tender or melancholy emotions."[8] In ancient Greece, pathos referred to "the quality of the transient or emotional, as opposed to the permanent or ideal."[9] One notion of pathos was primarily emotional suffering. There was, as yet, nothing pathological about pathos.

In the late 16th century, medical practitioners began to use the term *pathology* to refer to diseases in human physiology. By the 19th century, pathology became clearly anchored in the medical vocabulary as "the science or study of diseases" pertaining to the human body.[10] It is notable that in modern medicine, a pathologist works exclusively with "dead" tissue, whether cadavers or biopsy samples. In 1845 Todd and Bowman described pathology as "the physiology of disease,"[11] and more currently, it has been defined as the "study of deviations from normal structure, physiology, biochemistry, and cellular and molecular biology."[12] In one recent introductory work on pathology, the authors state the etymology of pathos as disease, completely obliterating its root meaning of suffering.[13]

The change of meaning from pathos as suffering to pathos as disease is not insignificant, for disease is medically defined as a "scientific, impersonal term"[14] and refers to "the consequences of a breakdown of the homeostatic control mechanisms."[15] Something intimately human and personal is replaced with something impersonal, a disease.

The re-definition of suffering as disease in medicine has its advantages and drawbacks; it is an investigation that is outside the scope of this book. However, in the study of the *psyche* (soul), emotion, and behavior, this re-definition has become especially problematic. Toward the middle of the 19th century, the emerging study of psychology borrowed the term pathology to refer to phenomena of the psyche or the mind. In 1842, Kingsley noted the importance of "understanding the pathology of the human soul, and [to] be able to cure its diseases."[16] The commonly used medical definition of pathology as the study of diseases of physiology and anatomy was handed over to psychology. The transfer of this definition from medicine becomes understandable in light of historical circumstances. Early psychology began studying physiology and neuroanatomy — a study directly influenced by the medical sciences — during the time of the school of Brücke-Helmholtz. As shown in Chapter 1, this tradition influenced Freud, and he continued to hope for a physiological reduction of psychological phenomena for as long as he lived.

The medical definition of pathology as the study of diseases implies the non-differentiation of mental or emotional suffering from disease. Just as with physiological disease, suffering disrupts a person's harmonious, homeostatic state of being. But disruption or breakdown of a harmonious state through emotional suffering does not, per *SE*, constitute a "negative" condition, a condition one must remove surgically or pharmacologically. By not differentiating emotional suffering from physiologically conditioned diseases, and their attendant suffering, the human phenomenon of suffering is not understood in its full complexity; it is *denied its full citizenship.*

Toward a Being-in-the-World
Understanding of Suffering

At its most basic, the being-in-the-world understanding of pathology takes into account and accepts the many different ways that humans can be in-the-world. Pathos belongs to these various manifestations of being-in. Pathos describes the human range and intensity of emotion and the suffering to which it is frequently connected.

Suffering forms an immensely complex phenomenon. It is a condition that the mental health profession refers to as mental or psychic suffering.[17] We must be conscious, that is, have subjective knowledge about the fact that we suffer. This knowledge is often expressed to the professional healer in the form of a complaint. This does not mean that we cannot suffer in silence or that we, at times, deny our suffering. But as far as modern therapeutics is concerned, it is the person's subjective reporting that something does not *feel* right that lets him or her seek professional counsel and treatment.

Human beings as beings-in-the-world are affected as much by world as by personal biology and history. We suffer from depression, anxiety, and panic attacks. But we also suffer from political oppression and ecological damage, as well as the paradoxes of life and living. Because we *are* our world, it is often difficult to ascertain if a mental paralysis, depression, or anxiety is due to conditions in a person's world, physiology, personal history, or a combination thereof.

Eric Cassell, physician and teacher at Cornell University School of Medicine, distinguishes between suffering and disease.[18] He writes about the importance for the physician to know the difference between suffering and disease because "[s]uffering is experienced by persons, not merely bodies, and has its source in challenges that threaten the intactness of the person as a complex social and psychological entity."[19] Perhaps Dr. Cassell's foremost dedication as a physician to help people in need does not permit him to discuss the potential qualities or benefits inherent in certain forms of suffering, because suffering constitutes one of the many ways we are-in-the-world. Suffering belongs to the realm of our possibilities. Rather than constituting merely a threat, suffering — as possibility — harbors in itself the potential and opportunity for each and every individual's life.

"Passion," the Latin word for suffering, highlights the complexity and ambiguity of suffering.[20] Passion refers to intense, strong emotions: an intensity that often overtakes an individual to such a degree that one speaks of a person being possessed by something. Yet, we do not generally regard passion as derogatory. To the contrary, a person who seems passionate about a cause often finds admiration. Similarly, two people passionately in love are appreciated for their excitement and the commitment they show each other. But our passions also can run away with us or blind us. This highlights the out-of-control aspect of passion, its intimate connection to suffering.

The complexity of suffering is related to the difficulty of ascertaining its etiology or origin. In the biomedical disease model of pathology, one assumes that the etiology lies in the physiological substrate of the individual. This explains why, at present, we speak about mental disease or illness as hormonal or chemical imbalance. In psychoanalytic parlance, psychological problems originate from fixations, insufficiently processed historical events, and givens of a person's childhood. The being-in-the-world understanding of an individual accepts the possibility of both physiological and historical origins of suffering and includes what I shall call the *worldly* aspect of suffering. In the following pages, I will highlight how human suffering and its possible manifestations in distress take on a broader, more encompassing meaning when understood from the perspective of being-in-the-world.

The Transpersonal Aspect of Suffering

The worldly aspect of pathology — pathology defined as "an understanding of suffering" — points to its transpersonal nature.[21] Our illness not only affects us, but also affects the world in which we live. Karl Baier uses the concept of the *Oikos* to refer to the reciprocal relationship between the ill person and his or her world.[22] Oikos signifies the Greek word for family, household, and home, as well as the inhabited universe (*oikoumenikos*). Home can refer to people's immediate surroundings as well as to their larger home, their workplace, community, city, and nation. Just as one can speak of the health or illness of an individual, so can one speak of a healthy or sick oikos.[23]

A healthy oikos is instrumental to our well-being. What we mean when we say that we feel good about ourselves refers not only to our own person but also to the oikos in which we live and work. Feeling good can indicate the confluence of a multiplicity of factors: we feel respected by our co-workers and supervisors, feel comfortable and safe in our home, can pursue our interests in solitude, have close friends nearby, are able to live in acceptable social and ecological conditions, have clean water and air, possess economic security, and so forth.

Conversely, our individual health or illness influences our oikos. Our absence from work due to illness can disrupt plans and may add additional burdens on our co-workers. Immediate family and friends concern themselves with us when we are ill, and they change their plans to be helpful. When we are healthy, our involvement and concern for the community can add to its stability and can give others and ourselves a heightened sense of safety and belonging.

Baier points out that an injury by itself, for example, does not lead to an illness. Rather, an injury only turns into an illness if the wound becomes infected, if the oikos, *micro-* and *macro-environments*, are not favorable and bacterial infection sets in. Understood this way, illness points to the bodily expression of a disturbed or disorderly oikos. Community physicians (note that the German word, *Hausarzt*, a physician who makes house calls, retains this idea of oikos) recognized the importance of the oikos for a person's health and made house calls. They routinely paid attention to the patient's oikos by *entering into* it. As part of their examination, they would listen to the patients' illness stories to understand the context of their suffering. In addition, the community physician would also take note of how patients' suffering affected those around them.[24]

Illness and Our World-Relation

As Heidegger points out, in our daily living we often seem unaware of how much we live embedded in the world and *with* others. We go about our habitual day-to-day affairs, and as long as we remain undisturbed and feel relatively good, we do not confront our worldliness — our interdependence with world and others. As shown in the last chapter, this interdependence reveals a certain ambiguity: our immersion in the world and our *essential* being-with-others makes possible our primordial understanding of world and others. It allows for communication and relating, as well as for many other day-to-day interactions.

It is important to remember that the ease of being-in-the-world afforded us, because of our fundamental relation with world and others (they), implies that human beings present themselves as foremost not themselves: "As they-self, the particular Dasein has been *dispersed* into the *they*, and must first find itself."[25] In other words, because we so easily forget our individual selves, it is possible for us to feel immersed in the world we inhabit.

This point might be somewhat counterintuitive at first, because forgetting our authentic selves actually allows us humans to be one with the world, so to speak. This implies that as we remember our authentic selves to some degree, we become alienated from the world in which we live. This is what Heidegger means when he writes about the *dispersion* of the human being in the they-self: "[the they] reveals itself as the 'Realest subject' of everydayness."[26] Because we humans tend to lose ourselves in the they-self of the everyday, illness or suffering can allow for the opportunity to remember that we belong in and relate to the world, to our oikos. As such, we are reminded of our authentic selves.

The worldly aspect of illness and suffering, therefore, leads us to recognize how oblivious we have been to our interdependence with the world. During illness, we perceive our in-the-worldness because people around us take notice and show concern for us. Our concept of *compassion*, of suffering with, expresses this phenomenon.[27] Not only other fellow beings, but also the physical world becomes pronounced. We now notice the world of the hospital or clinic within the community, the network of emergency care provisions, pharmacies, and offices of specialized care. In this way, our illness forces us to remember our relation to the world and other beings-in-the-world.

In our being-ill, we do not only rediscover our connection with and to the world; those who experience an illness and those who suffer with them recognize, as Baier remarks, the *unum neccessarium* that constitutes the essential for us in our lives.[28] We re-evaluate wishes, goals, or hopes in light of the experience of suffering or illness. This re-evaluation can lead us to a re-thinking of our own being. It also may lead to a re-thinking of our past and future projects and of the premises and assumptions guiding our lives. This deliberation and imagining of changes, leading into different directions and to paths not trodden, show how illness and suffering can allow for a renewed questioning of the essential elements of life.

A poignant example of this is found in Ivan Illych who, in much pain, questions himself: "'Can it be that I have not lived as one ought?' suddenly came into his head."[29]

Suffering as Heightened Sensitivity to Ontic Questions in Daily Life

The experience of suffering allows for a deeper understanding of oneself as being-in-the-world. This deepening of understanding through suffering emphasizes what Alice Holzhey-Kunz has named "the ambiguous nature of human suffering."[30] Following Heidegger, she points out that human beings live foremost in a realm where they do not live their authentic selves. One may call this realm a place where humans unconsciously accept the validity of common sense and tradition.[31] This place of the everyday is a space where one can find comfort and shelter from the demands of one's own having-to-be. When we become aware of how comfortable and inauthentic we have been, we may realize that the comfort we found was at the expense of being and living our own possibilities.

As an example of this phenomenon, Holzhey-Kunz relates how the realization of one's denial can lead to a suffering of psyche. At the turn of the 19th century, women faced an unsolvable dilemma. Living at a time when society expounded the goals and values of individual expression, women remained bound to traditional views and incapable of translating those ideals into the concrete. This bind led many women to what the psychoanalyst of that day diagnosed as *hysteria*, a condition often associated with a variety of conversion symptoms and conversion reaction.[32] Holzhey-Kunz links this phenomenon to the awareness of fin de siècle women, to their ability to be sensitive (whether consciously or unconsciously) to the paradoxical situation given by the socio-historic circumstances. Those circumstances promised emancipation but resisted its implementation.[33]

Following this argument, Holzhey-Kunz conceptualizes suffering as the state of "heightened sensibility to the basic conditions of being-in-the-world."[34] These basic conditions encompass our finality or our mortality. Our finality, in turn, determines the frame of our existence. Within it, we face issues of understanding the meaning of our own being and confront questions of our belonging in and to the world. We experience anxieties that point to our limitations and possibilities and to those given by our historicity. This meditation upon the fundamentals of our existence, initiated through our heightened sensitivity to the basic conditions of being-in-the-world caused by suffering, contributes to becoming what Holzhey-Kunz calls a "*philosopher* against *intention* [*Philosoph* wider *Willen*]."[35] This means that even those of us who resist any probing of our meaning and purpose in life can be pushed to such questioning through anxieties and fears that might suddenly befall us.

People suffer from their heightened sensibility to fundamental human conditions or truths. What they face in their day-to-day living has acquired deeper meaning: experiences and encounters of everyday life, however small or trivial, remind us of larger and more significant ontological questions and truths. What used to belong to the relatively small problems of the everyday now points to larger issues of life and living. We begin to continually question the deeper meaning of our existence as triggered by day-to-day events. But this questioning can present a heavy burden and can become a source of suffering in itself. This is an important point because it speaks to the suffering that can arise from seeking answers to the larger questions of life. Seeking can urge one to a philosophical stance toward life not often supported in our societies. Such philosophical questioning, common among artistic persons, often results in great human achievements, which make society more aware of its own insufficiencies. So, in some cases, this reflection not only has a personal benefit but serves the greater good as well. In the words of Rollo May in his *The Courage to Create*: "We cannot escape our anxiety over the fact that the artists, together with creative persons of all sorts, are the possible destroyers of our nicely ordered system."[36] Without such dismantling of our nicely ordered systems, change and advancement cannot occur.

The suffering person, having left the insensitivity of the they-self and of tradition, has also left behind the comfort that they-self and tradition provide. The questioner who experiences an ongoing sensitivity to the ontological dimension of everyday experiences suffers under the burden she or he carries. We speak of her as carrying the "pain of the world" (*Weltschmerz*), of being melancholic. This points to the difference between the unintentional philosopher and one who goes about philosophy deliberately. For example, a woman who suffers from her meaningful daily encounters stands in contrast to the intentional philosopher sitting in her book-lined office. The latter chooses to *focus on an issue* and tries not to allow distractions of the many concrete details of the everyday, whereas the former feels overwhelmed by the many everyday issues that she confronts.[37]

Holzhey-Kunz states that the continual assignment of meaning to the events of daily living can interfere with one's living with oneself and others. An utter sensitivity to listen to one's being can lead to an inability to act at all because fundamental human issues demand all the attention. This preoccupation does not permit an acknowledgment of the positive things that happen during one's day, the things that *do* work. The high standards that these questioners have often set themselves — standards that can never be achieved — can also lead to an indifference to the lighter, positive things of life.

Sensitivity to the world means sensitivity to the paradoxical nature of the human condition, to the insoluble antinomies of life. Because one finds these conditions unacceptable, one tries to find solutions to them. But these problems do not lend themselves to solutions. What leads someone to suffer, therefore, constitutes the unwillingness to accept the basic human condition. Such a person may express her or his suffering by choosing to withdraw from the world, or she may want to isolate herself from the people around her. Doing so, she alienates herself, a state that increases her burden and suffering even further. Imagine living in a world where suffering was not marginalized, but rather integrated as a normal, acceptable part of life. In such a world, we might not feel the need to retreat or withdraw.

One's sensitivity for the *ontic* dimension of life, for one's own possibilities, does not necessarily lead to a spiral of self-limiting suffering. The basic difference between the psychic sufferer and one able to use her or his sensitivity for a deeper understanding of self and living would indicate that the latter can accept the mysterious quality of being. Just as important, accepting the basic human condition also relates to accepting the fact that humans cannot linger continually in the realm of the ontological without facing the consequences of feeling separate from others and the world around them. As beings-in-the-world, the ontic realm of existence discloses an important part and mode of who we are. It constitutes part of our home. We belong to the world of the everyday as much as to the ontological realm of timeless truths. Suffering has citizenship in this world; it is a part of our home.

Psychopathology, Suffering, and Creativity

Suffering is part of who and how we are in the world. As a multifaceted phenomenon, it can restrict and limit the way we live in the world, or it can provide us with an opportunity for living our given possibilities more fully. Rilke has called suffering and pain our ground, the place of living.[38] Nietzsche saw it as a gift, an opportunity for reflection.[39] In Heideggerian terms, pathos points to one's understanding that the public or they-self does not offer the fulfillment it *appears* to hold. Pathos insists on the discovery of the possibilities of one's *own* being, a discovery that can encompass facing one's anxieties and feelings of guilt.[40]

The discovery of one's possibilities constitutes a creative process because my possibilities are unique and belong to me only. Popular conceptualizations of the suffering artist or the mad poet express the close link between suffering and the creative process. The connection between human creativity and suffering is highly complex and often romanticized. Nevertheless, even a brief look at this helps us to understand the phenomenon of human suffering from a being-in-the-world perspective. This will broaden modern therapeutics' narrow and undifferentiated conception of suffering as something foreign or separate from the human being, a conception that insists on understanding suffering as a unilaterally negative experience.

In the last few decades, researchers have tried to understand the link between psychopathology — in its modern-day usage: emotional or mental illness — and artistic creativity.[41] A study of manic-depressive illness revealed significant data correlating the illness with exceptional artistic and mathematical abilities.[42] Similar results were obtained in a study on patients diagnosed as cyclothymic and manic-depressive.[43] More recently, A. M. Ludwig completed an extensive research project that specifically attempted "to determine the relationship between creative activity and psychopathology."[44] Ludwig sampled 1,005 individuals selected by a review of their biographies in *The New York Times Book Review* of the last 30 years. He also tried to understand whether individuals of certain creative professions showed a higher rate of mental disturbance than those in other, less creative professions. Ludwig found that

> [t]hose in the creative arts not only experience emotional difficulties earlier in life and over a longer time span but they also display greater rates of alcoholism, drug abuse, depression, mania, somatic problems, anxiety, psychoses, and adjustment disorders and, consequently, undergo most forms of psychiatric therapy more often.[45]

Ludwig summarizes "that members of the theatrical profession, all categories of writers, artists but not architects/designers, and musical performers and composers experience significantly more psychiatric difficulties over the course of their lives in comparison mostly to public officials, military personnel, social scientists, physical scientists, and, in some instances, businessmen."[46] Ludwig comments that his results raise "the question as to whether the existence of certain forms of psychopathology may be advantageous for certain professions."[47] In raising this question he gives significant support for the thesis that for those who are aware, the constitutionality of being-in-the-world includes suffering. The issue raised by Ludwig, as to the relationship between psychopathology and creativity, is a most unusual but important one. In the context of modern therapeutics, can psychopathology — defined as mental illness or disorder — be "advantageous for certain professions"? It appears that the question this research raises, a question that links psychopathology with its potential benefits, requires a redefinition of what exactly psychopathology means. But Ludwig does not deal with the conceptual issues that his question raises. Instead, he circumvents the problem via reformulation: "[t]he more appropriate issue seems to be what types of psychopathology, if any, tend to be associated with certain professions, and with what degree of creative achievement within these professions, and during what time periods in these individuals' lives."[48]

To restate the research results as such obviates the need for a fundamental re-evaluation of the concept of psychopathology as mental disorder. Ludwig sidesteps the central issue. Instead, he maintains the standard definition of mental disorder and associates it with certain professions. To link some professions more than others with personality disorders seems appropriate at first glance only. Essentially, it implies that certain personality characteristics seem more conducive than others for success in a professional field. Why, then, should we regard these personality traits as mental "disorder" if they seem essential not only for the individuals' creative expressions, their being-in-the-worldness, but also for their very success in their profession? Why should we not regard these personality traits as advantageous and point out the advantages to the sufferers? How do we know or judge when to treat mental disorder and when not to? What are the implications for the definition of (psycho)pathology as a mental disorder in need of treatment?

Kay Jamison raises these questions in "Mood Disorders and Patterns of Creativity in British Writers and Artists."[49] Sampling eminent British writers and artists, Jamison wants "to study differences in subgroups (poets, novelists, playwrights, biographers, artists); to examine seasonal patterns of moods and productivity; and to inquire into the perceived role of very intense moods in the writers' and artists' work."[50] Jamison notes that affective illness in this sample of British writers and artists "is strikingly high."[51] Nevertheless, the results, so the author notes, compare to those of other studies.[52] She summarizes the link between mental disturbance and the creative individual:

> *Profound changes in mood, cognition, personality, sleep, energy and behavior characterize both altered mood and creative states. Cognitive changes occurring during hypomanic states — e.g., the increase in speed, associational fluency and flexibility of thought — are likewise critical to creativity. For writers and artists, who draw so deeply from their lives and emotions for their work, the wide range, intensity, fluctuation and variability of emotional experience brought about by mood disorders can work to the advantage, as well as disadvantage, of original composition. Too, what hypomania generates in enthusiasm and excess, the more critical and obsessive eye of depression often effectively judges and edits.[53]*

Commenting on her study's results, Jamison addresses the implications of the significant association between mental illness and creativity. Specifically, she validates the concern of many artists and writers that psychiatric treatment, especially treatment based on medication, can interfere with creativity and productivity. She notes, cautiously, that "not all of these fears are realistic, but some may be."[54] This doubt regarding the treatment of a diagnosed mental illness leads Jamison to advocate new guidelines that assess the appropriateness of treatment on a case-by-case basis. She wants the professional to pay more attention to the positive aspects of mood disorders (but also to potential detrimental consequences such as suicide and severe depression), to the possible harmful effects of medication on the creative process, and to the impact of seasonal patterns on mood disturbances. She concludes that the close connection between mood disorders and creativity shown in her study also has potential societal implications. Referring to the present advances in genetic research, which promise the early treatment of certain mental disorders, Jamison cautions that individual and societal benefits and costs of these treatments require careful consideration.

My brief excursion into the complex issue of creativity highlights the limitations of the dominant understanding of pathology as mental illness or disease. As I have shown, this definition reveals the ambiguous nature of (psycho)pathology. It seems advantageous, even as it is also debilitating. To pay tribute to the inherent complexity of pathology, it may be beneficial to return to the original meaning of pathology as the study of suffering. This understanding acknowledges the multifaceted nature of pathology and essential role in how human beings live in the world. A statement by F. Barron, who conducted a comprehensive study on creativity in the 1950s summarizes the importance of disorder and its equivocal nature for being human:

> [C]reative individuals are most at home with complexity
> and apparent disorder than other people are. . . . The
> creative individual in his generalized preference for

apparent disorder, turns to the dimly realized life of the unconscious, and is likely to have more than the usual amount of respect for the forces of the irrational in himself and in others . . . . [T]he creative individual not only respects the irrational in himself, but courts it as the most promising source of novelty in his own thought. He rejects the demand of society that he should shun in himself the primitive, the uncultured, the naive, the magical, the nonsensical; that he must be a "civilized" member of the community. When an individual thinks in ways which are customarily tabooed, his fellows may regard him as mentally unbalanced. In my view this kind of imbalance is more likely to be healthy than unhealthy. The truly creative individual stands ready to abandon old classifications and to acknowledge that life, particularly his own unique life, is rich with new possibilities. To him, disorder offers the potentiality of order.[55]

Let us now turn to an actual case study to clarify his point.

The Case of Dr. Cobling

Medard Boss, a psychiatrist strongly influenced by phenomenological/existential therapy and especially by Heidegger's Daseinsanalysis, describes the following case of a Dr. Cobling.[56] Boss considers this case seminal, because not only was it the catalyst for a radical change in his practice of psychotherapy, but it also altered his philosophical stance. Dr. Cobling, a 36-year-old German woman, a psychiatrist herself, grew up in a rigidly controlled household that expounded the values of hard work and "demanded unremitting self-denial and sacrifice to duty."[57] She subsequently worked her way up to the directorship of a psychiatric hospital, which, because of her gender, was a feat of immense effort. When Dr. Cobling entered therapy, she arrived on the verge of a collapse. She suffered from a high level of anxiety, obvious in the tremor of her hands and the wide dilation of her pupils; she experienced self-destructive impulses and suicidal ideation.[58]

She not only saw strange faces looking at her during broad daylight, but she also heard sounds differently. Normal noises and voices seemed exaggerated to her and took on bizarre, sometimes frightening meanings. In the beginning of therapy, Boss appeared eager to point out to Dr. Cobling that these phenomena presented just hallucinations without any reality and related to a "disturbed metabolism in the brain tissues," a fact that corresponded to an analysis of Dr. Cobling's EEG. But the patient dismissed the therapist's naturalistic explanations and became rather furious. She criticized him for speaking "utter psychological nonsense" and of possessing no understanding of the nature of "non-hallucinatory reality." She accused him of hiding behind words. Challenged, Boss reports that he re-read various psychological theories to see if he could find answers to the nature of reality, the subject, and the person, all to no avail.[59]

Healing Potential of Acknowledging Subjective Reality

It was Boss's prior exposure to the philosophy of Daseinsanalysis that allowed for a different view of Dr. Cobling and her hallucinatory delusions. Instead of assuming the existence of certain drives or unconscious forces and understanding the patient's experiences as pathogenic, Boss began to address Dr. Cobling's reality and to see her hallucinations and delusions as something that *approached* her: "Something is sent to her, seeks admission to her awareness and appearance therein. It is something of her future that approaches her, comes to meet her, seeks to be included in her present. This something for this patient is pre-eminently the realm of phenomena that reveals itself in the bodily-erotic ways of human relating to the world."[60] These insights changed the way Boss proceeded in his therapy. Rather than "hiding behind words," Boss acknowledged the patient's reality:

You are perfectly right. There is no sense in granting one reality priority over another. It would be quite futile for us to maintain that this table before us is more real than your motorcycling spies merely because they elude my perception and are perceptible only to you. Why don't we let them stand as the phenomena they reveal themselves to be? Then there is only one thing worth our attention. That is to consider the full meaning-content of that which discloses itself to us. If you keep meeting spies at every turn, and a psychiatrist were to attempt to reduce these perceptions to fictitious hallucinations or figments of your imagination, to impute only a psychic reality to them as projections out of your unconscious, then I would agree with you completely that he would be taking in quite meaning-less terms which are not promoting our understanding of your experiences in the least.[61]

The therapist's acceptance of the patient's reality — his validation of her hallucinations as part of her personal reality — led to astounding improvements in her therapy. This improvement, however, did not have the face of more socially accepted behavior. Not ever having been permitted to be a child and to enjoy the carefree life associated with childhood, she now played and painted with her feces, or smeared her whole body with them in the bathtub. She would arrive with a baby bottle at the analytic hour and have her therapist feed her. At the same time, she showed herself much more unrestrained and open in her work and private life, and started to develop a social life as she felt more liberated in her contact with others. But the imprint of so many years of self-denial were not easily overcome, and Dr. Cobling, with her newly established order as yet too fragile to withstand much outside pressure, collapsed again. Late at night the therapist received a phone call from Dr. Cobling, in which she told him that felt like "ripping her belly open with a big knife, that she wants to cut her arteries and suck her own blood." The therapist hurried to the patient's house:

> *"How could anybody get better," the therapist asks reassuringly, "without the old neurotic world collapsing in the process? It is far too narrow and rigid to survive. And if this sort of destruction of the old neurotic prison is happening to you, is that really so dreadful? To be so filled with apprehension as you are, and to hear nothing but death and destruction on every hand, can only mean one is still imprisoned in the error of believing one's own neurotic egocentric world to be the sole possibility of existence and that when this shows signs of cracking, it means the crack of doom. For the real, essential being that is you, what is happening now is far from being an end. It is merely a chance taking place in its way of appearing."*[62]

In the next few weeks Dr. Cobling regressed again during her therapy sessions and let herself be fed with the baby bottle. A disturbing, incestuous dream with her father, coupled with emerging feelings for her therapist, threw her back into a crisis. In addition, she acknowledged that she was trying to cheat the little girl inside by playing the grown-up doctor. One day she felt so good about herself that she bought new clothes to make herself feel more attractive. But outside the clothing store, she saw a man writing in a note-pad and feared that he would tell the police about her intentions. Haunted by auditory hallucinations, she ran back home. In the next analytic hour she engaged in some three dimensional modeling with clay[63]:

> *At first she was obliged to model a female figure in the form of a rigid crucifix. Still, as soon as it was finished, it transformed itself (seemingly spontaneously in her hands) into a graceful dancing girl. Over and over, the cross and dancer contended with one another for a place in her world. How could she solve this conflict in the medium of earthen clay? The solution came only much later in a meditative exercise devised by Dr. Cobling herself, when she suddenly realized that God pervades everything, even a whore dancer.*[64]

The case of Dr. Cobling does not end here but reaches a significant new phase as she attempts to broaden the confines of her world. This enlargement rests on the insight of the necessity of both disorder and pain without which order, stability, harmony, and even an understanding of order itself, cannot be possible.[65]

The Question Concerning Diagnosis

Diagnosis lies at the heart of therapeutics. In this way clinicians assess the person seeking help. Boss had titled his encounter with Dr. Cobling "the patient who made him see differently." His engagement shows that the way clinicians diagnose reveals how they conceptualize their patients' distress. *The Textbook of Psychiatry* formulates the centrality of diagnosis as follows:

> *The patient is a suffering person who is seeking help and relief. The psychiatrist is a medical expert in psychiatric diagnosis and treatment and in interpersonal relationships. The patient reveals what is troubling him in the context of a confidential patient-doctor relationship. The psychiatrist listens and makes responses that are geared toward obtaining as clear an understanding of the patient's problems as possible. The psychiatrist encourages a free-flowing exchange of information between himself and patient. The psychiatrist arrives at a diagnostic formulation of the patient's problems at the conclusion of the interview. The more accurate the diagnostic assessment, the more appropriate is the treatment planning.*[66]

Following this definition, diagnosis appears as an uncontroversial, matter-of-fact procedure. However, arguments regarding the value of diagnosis in therapeutics vary. Some practitioners claim that without a clear diagnostic system, therapeutic knowledge and communication is impossible among professionals, while others believe that current diagnostics do more harm than good by not allowing the clinician to fully see the client. This debate has persisted for two centuries. In 1822, the English alienist Prichard, for instance, wrote that it seemed "preposterously absurd" to classify diseases and pretend to have established order in what was principally disorder. The most noted early critic of traditional diagnostics before the nascence of the anti-psychiatry movement in the 1960s was Karl Menninger. His questioning of the value of diagnosis goes back to the 1940s. In the late 1950s, Menninger wrote that diagnosis

> is always a complex set of statements — descriptive, analytic and evaluative. They have to describe a patient's method of interacting with his environment, past and present. We examine the environment as well as the patient, and the psychiatric diagnosis is always both polydimensional and multidisciplinary. Furthermore, a psychiatric diagnosis is always continuous and changing. Theoretically, it cannot be recorded, because no sooner has a description been entered upon a case record than it begins to be out of date.[67]

R. E. Kendell is one of the more prolific writers on the issues surrounding diagnosis.[68] He considers the classification of mental illness inevitable and points out that clients can be grouped into three categories: (1) those who display the same symptoms as other psychiatric clients, (2) those who share symptoms with a subset of the total client population, and (3) those who present problems unique to themselves. It seems pointless to classify clients from the first and last group, given that these groups contain large numbers of people — every client would either have the same diagnosis or would possess their own unique one. However, what Kendell states about the second and third client groups constitutes a most interesting argument. He admits that the second group of patients appears "considerably smaller for mental illness than it is for physical illness, but," he continues, "our attention still has to be focused on category two if we are ever to increase in knowledge and understanding."[69] Kendell rightly stresses that we all, clinicians or laypersons, tend to classify people more or less automatically by searching for known features in others that help us in understanding them. Yet, Kendell's attempt to guard the value of classification for mental illnesses reaches hyperbole, as in the following passage:

> [I]nsofar as every patient is unique it becomes impossible to acquire any useful knowledge. In the course of treating an individual patient we may well learn important things about him and become better able to help him as a result. But that knowledge and skill will be of no use in treating other patients because they will be quite different. If our patients really differed from one another in their most important characteristics, it would be impossible to learn anything useful from teachers, colleagues, or textbooks, or even from our own experience. After 30 years in practice we would be no

better equipped to help our next patient than the day we entered medical school . . . if all patients were really quite different from one another, all learning and all useful communication would be impossible.[70]

In effect, Kendell argues that a system of classifying mental illnesses is essential. Without it, clinicians would be unable to understand their clients and would be *condemned* to treat every new experience as the first one. The argument deserves close scrutiny. Knowledge and "all useful communication" is only possible if it is classifiable.[71] The corollary is that only what is classifiable can be "usefully communicated" and constitutes knowledge.[72] Does this attitude imply that artists cannot communicate any useful knowledge to their audiences unless this knowledge is first classified through an existing taxonomy? Does it mean that experience, unless categorized, has no useful value for clinical praxis? Or does the intuitive hunch — that most clinicians reluctantly admit guides their search for understanding — not qualify as knowledge? A definition that equates knowledge with classifiability is a parochial understanding of knowledge. It leaves unexamined the very base or source of knowledge, the knowledge that makes classification possible in the first place. What is *that* knowledge that creates and questions classification? What knowledge allows for self-reflection? In answering these questions we should consider Nietzsche's statement that "the biggest fable of all is the fable of knowledge,"[73] or T. S. Eliot's query, "Where is the wisdom we have lost in knowledge?"[74]

AMBIGUITY OF SUFFERING

Beyond Classification

Classified knowledge constitutes *one* valuable source of knowledge when used in conjunction with other modes of knowing and understanding. Before clinicians can classify their clients, they must learn about them. This learning requires an ability to adequately perceive clients. However, perception is always not only theory driven but theory informed, that is, known theories inform and limit the perceiver only to the possibilities the theory acknowledges. Therefore, the question is not whether clinicians should diagnose their clients. Diagnosis as "the art of identifying a disease from its signs and symptoms"[75] remains necessary for any kind of therapeutic treatment. It constitutes an important aspect of therapeutics. But at issue here is the degree to which clinicians are aware of *how* they *perceive* the client, or *how* they *interpret* the signs and symptoms and link them to *their* conception of disease or illness.

The issue of perception as it enters diagnostics becomes obvious in the various studies testing the reliability and validity of diagnoses. Kendell notes that "the crucial failing of psychiatric diagnoses, the one that led to widespread disillusionment with the whole business of diagnosis, was their failure to determine treatment and predict outcome."[76] He adds that the results of dozens of studies testing the reliability of diagnoses "were almost uniformly depressing."[77] Why defend the traditional psychiatric classifications of mental illnesses? To return to Kendell again, he believes that the last decades of the drug treatment revolution, combined with the insights of behavior therapists and geneticists, have established a clearer differentiation between various mental illnesses. These new developments give rise to Kendell's optimism that the "debate about whether diagnoses are appropriate or necessary in psychiatry . . . is no longer a live issue today. . . . Those who urged psychiatry to abandon its diagnoses were misguided and have been repudiated."[78] Once again we can see how deeply the mechanistic understanding of the human being (mis)guides Kendell and his colleagues in their professional pursuits.

Psychiatric Diagnosis and Worldliness

The question concerning diagnosis has been complicated further by the "discovery" of a variable that psychotherapeutics hitherto has neglected in its theory and practice: culture. Psychiatrist Arthur

Kleinman remains instrumental in bringing the issue of the importance of culture in therapeutics to the foreground. Kleinman summarizes the significance of culture for therapeutics:

> *Culture holds importance for psychiatry, in my view, principally because it brings a special kind of criticism to bear on research regarding mental illness and treatment. From the cross-cultural perspective, the fundamental questions in psychiatry — how to distinguish the normal from the abnormal; how disorder is perceived, experienced, and expressed; why treatments succeed or fail; indeed the purposes and scope of psychiatry itself — are all caught up in a reciprocal relationship between the social world of the person and his body/self (psychobiology).*[79]

Asking the question of what constitutes a psychiatric diagnosis, Kleinman points out that diagnostic categories often indicate the "outcomes of historical developments, cultural influences, and political negotiations."[80] Indeed, he feels that psychiatric taxonomies may be part of an increasing trend to medicalize social problems. Drawing on recent cross-cultural research combined with his own therapeutic experiences in China, Kleinman shows that cultural norms and expectations as well as social conditions significantly affect changes in a person's psychobiology. Kleinman also points to recent research that indicates the degree to which "most disorders — including a wide range of medical disorders — have their highest prevalence rate among the poor and disadvantaged."[81] Personal coping skills, social stresses, and individuals' available support (interpersonal and economic) systems, all contribute to the onset of a disorder. But even this conceptualization, according to Kleinman, trivializes the social historical realities in which people in distress find themselves. In a study on patients in chronic pain, he and his colleagues found that "ethnographic description of the local life worlds of patients made for more valid understanding of the course of complaints and disability than psychometric measures of stress, supports, and coping."[82]

Menninger, in an almost uncanny fashion, intuited decades earlier the present-day insights of cross-cultural research. He also took note of the effects of economics and social conditions on mental disorders that Kleinman brings together to re-think medicine and psychiatry. Writing in 1948, Menninger asks the question:

> *What shall we call the disease represented by a man who has always been frail but has worked very hard to support his widowed mother, did not feel he could afford to get married, busies himself in the details of a complicated job, develops paralyzing headaches, loses time at the office for which pay is deducted from his wages, worries about this so much that he loses sleep and begins vomiting after each meal? What is the diagnosis in a patient who has coronary symptoms whenever he takes his wife to a party? Or in a woman who has*

a migraine on the weekends that her son is home from college? [83]

Biopsychiatry overlooks humans' worldliness by diagnosing mental disorder in terms of biology. Psychoanalysis and most other psychotherapies overlook humans' worldliness by emphasizing the intrapsychic origins of mental disorder. This oversight has led to a perception of the human being that does injustice to the complex realities of life in a mysterious world. These therapies reduce clients' problems to biology or internal mechanisms of the psyche while they neglect the complex interaction and interdependence between world and individual, between cosmos and psyche.

The concluding chapter deals with the extra-therapeutic factors that might account for the neglect of an approach to therapy informed by a more adequate description of human beings and their challenges. It also examines a way of thinking that allows for the continual enlarging of our understanding of what it means to be human.

Specifically, I return to the central question of this book: Why does a phenomenon based on a mechanistic model of the human being, such as informs biopsychiatry, have the capacity to attract such a large following? Why has it enjoyed such a widespread resurgence?

CHAPTER 5

Money and Power: Back to a Reductionist View of a Human Being

You see, we slip back, without knowing it, from our progress, into something we did not intend: where we become caught up, as in a dream, and where we die without waking.

— RAINER MARIA RILKE

The Question: What Makes the Positivist Approach so Attractive?

Why does the positivist understanding of the human being continue its reign within contemporary therapeutic culture? What continues to make this paradigm attractive despite many obvious limitations? Although we are now in the 21st century, the positivist approach to the treatment of human suffering continues to dominate the theoretical foundation of present-day biopsychiatry and many psychoanalytically influenced psychotherapies.[1] My approach to this question will highlight the often-ignored *worldly* influences that impinge on the way the practitioner makes decisions — one that is frequently at odds with what would constitute a far more comprehensive *quality of care* for the person in need.

Psychotherapeutics as an enterprise is driven not only by concepts and theories but also by tools, economics, politics, and institutions.[2] As such, it falls under the sway of a plethora of extra-therapeutic factors at odds with the *therapeutic spirit*. This refers to the provision of optimal, *empathic patient care*.[3] Here, I will delineate the economic and political dimensions that shape the way in which people who need psychotherapeutic care are treated. Within the economic dimension, I will focus on the inordinate influence that the psychopharmaceutical industry and the phenomenon of managed care, with its concomitant bureaucratization, have on the care of people in psychic distress.

Back to Pre-Freudian Days

Half a century of a psychoanalytically influenced psychiatry and psychotherapy has spawned a seemingly endless therapeutic repertoire through family, existential, cognitive, and systems therapies. Yet the contemporary treatment modalities with their conventional wisdom have yielded a practice of psychotherapeutics more similar to the reductionist approach to mental health, which was typical in the days of Freud. This approach conceptualizes mental illness as a disease of the brain; thus, it quite naturally adheres to traditional medical model thinking. By its adherence to this thinking, the psychiatric culture in the West has effectively reinvented the medical wheel in its own laboratory. This misses the mark of the very definition of quality of care that the Institute of Medicine has established for itself: namely, to provide care that "should reflect appropriate use of the most current knowledge about scientific, clinical, technical, interpersonal, manual, cognitive, and organizational and management elements of health care."[4]

The appropriate use of the most current knowledge, however, implies the very acknowledgment of many different and important discoveries of the 20th century:

∞ We possess evidence of the interdependency of human beings with their world.

∞ We now understand the importance of socio-politico-environmental and cultural factors in the mental health of an individual.

∞ We know the danger of singular truth claims — that is, of the existence of exclusive expert knowledge with respect to the subjective human realm.

❧ We have shown the multi-causality and inherent complexity of human phenomena, especially concerning human emotions and behavior.

❧ We have come to understand the patient's fundamental need for care that reaches beyond technical intervention.

❧ We have shown clearly through the advances in phenomenological philosophy and quantum physics that we live in a perceiver-dependent world, a world where our perception influences the perceived and the perceived influences the perceiver.

As I have mentioned, a psychotherapeutics that returns to the major tenets of the traditional medical model reverts to those attitudes typical of the mechanistic view of the human being.

As such, psychotherapeutics neglects to heed vital contemporary treatment modalities and does not fully provide quality of care. There are many explanations for the neglect of the current status of knowledge with respect to mental health care. I believe that these explanations derive principally from the political and economic realm. Together, political and economic factors circumscribe issues of status and power with respect to the psychiatric and psychotherapeutic professions. As respectable and fundable sciences, these issues are linked also to the personal status and power of the mental health professional. Economic factors mandate the need for cost-efficient/cost-containing treatments of peoples' mental health issues, as demanded by corporate and public institutions and insurance companies. These considerations have influenced the forging of various alliances between mental health practitioners and private and public organizations. Further, these alliances have helped return the theoretical conceptualizations and practice of mental health to a simplistic and mechanistic understanding of mental distress that is *disembodied* from the world.

I summarize the effect this return has on mental health care as follows:

  ∽ There is a basic misunderstanding of the dimensions of human suffering.

  ∽ Socio-political difficulties are conceptualized (and therefore, simplified) as medical problems.

  ∽ There is a disregard for the cultural variability of mental distress and illness (as exemplified by the rigidity of the DSM categories of mental illness).

  ∽ There is a lack of comprehensive, inclusive, and authentically imaginative research in regard to the fundamental issues involved in care.

  ∽ The psychiatric culture misses key dimensions with respect to patients in need of care, resulting in a damaging denial of the patient's *rich* world.

ॐ Patients' lives and vitalities are endangered through the side-effects and overuse of psychopharmaceuticals.

ॐ There is a maze of bureaucracy now common to mental health care, a system that results in vital medical and psychotherapeutic decisions based on cost, codes, and regulations, rather than on professional assessment of patients' needs.

Present-day psychotherapeutics are principally driven, not by the needs of the person seeking help, but by professional interests that are connected to market forces rather than therapeutic concerns. These two facets of the argument are interdependent; that is, an oversimplified understanding of the human being makes possible the bureaucratization of mental health care. Simultaneously, this increased bureaucratization helps entrench further the oversimplified understanding of the human being.

The growing body of research describing the history of the treatment of the mentally ill and distressed is troubling in itself.[5] Nevertheless, highlighting past attempts to reduce mental distress to a physiological basis, with corresponding treatment, will help the reader orient current vogues of treatment into a historical context. Also, it will serve as a reminder of the damaging treatments to which the so-called mentally distressed are routinely subjected within the guise of the medical model.

Tuke's Reform in the 18th Century
and the Reaction of the Medical World

In his book, *One Hundred Years of Psychiatry*, highly respected author Emil Kraeplin details some of the more regrettable methods used by the medical establishment and, later, the psychiatric establishment to "cure" the "mentally insane."[6] "Therapeutic" approaches of the day included somewhat benign and useless methods, like blood-letting, to the more injurious practice of immersing patients in freezing water. These methods were employed to re-establish medical authority in the treatment of the mentally distressed. This authority was in the process of serious erosion in the late 18th century when the English businessman William Tuke, a lay practitioner, spearheaded successful asylum reform. Tuke's strategy was founded on the premise that those suffering from mental distress should be treated in a manner that was both humane and compassionate. With this model driving his reforms, Tuke reintroduced the psychologically traumatized to a compassionate environment, and, in so doing, alleviated the systemic distress that had become their way of life. Tuke was appalled by the harsh and frequently brutal remedies to which those deemed mentally infirm were routinely subjected. His concept of moral treatment focused on providing the psychologically and emotionally weary with a warm, homelike environment that paid specific attention to respectful treatment of patients. But Tuke's asylum reform had placed laypeople in charge instead of medical doctors. The medical establishment became anxious to reassert its power.[7]

Unable to prove that any of their physical treatments could actually provide palliative results for their patients, psychiatrists used their political power and influence to help defeat the many reform bills initiated by Tuke's asylum reform movement. These bills, introduced from 1810 through the 1820s, potentially could have led to a relinquishment of medical practitioners' control over the treatment of the "mentally infirm." To further stabilize the position of the medical establishment, "from about 1815 onwards, a veritable spate of books and articles purporting to be medical treatises on the treatment of insanity began to appear."[8] But moral treatment under Tuke's leadership was loathe to develop an ideological treatment rationale of the stripe common to the medical establishment. This made it vulnerable to attack from an intellectual environment that demanded scientific evidence to back claims of efficacy. By the mid-1840s, control of most asylums shifted back to the hands of medical personnel.

AMBIGUITY OF SUFFERING

Toward Unquestionable Authority
of Medical Practitioners

Introduced to the public in 1848, the *Journal of Psychological Medicine and Mental Pathology* was the first journal of its kind to deal specifically with "insanity." This was quickly followed, in 1853, by a second journal titled *Asylum Journal*. The emphasis of both journals was that "[i]nsanity is purely a disease of the brain. The physician is now the responsible guardian of the lunatic and must ever remain so."[9] Michael Clark supports the above analysis and shows the parallelism between American and European psychiatry in the 19th century. He finds "that the last four decades of the century were characterized by a growing preponderance of somatic-pathological approaches to almost every aspect of *psychological medicine*, and by a corresponding tendency to disparage any kind of psychological approach to the problems of mental disorder."[10] Clark points out that this "emphatic rejection of the psychological interpretation" of mental illness was largely due to "the history of medicine's appropriation and cultivation of mental disorder as part of its rightful and 'natural' sphere of professional involvement."[11] As I have detailed in Chapter 1, emotions and mental processes were reduced, without question, to physiology. Furthermore, because mental disorders were equated with weaknesses of the will — especially when physical treatments showed little effect — medical practitioners understood their professional responsibility in terms of enforcing the patient's "compliance and submission" to their authority. Physicians felt their assertion of moral authority was therapeutically indicated, thus making their moral authority not only a virtue but also a treatment necessity. This assertion of authority served the purpose of "the repression of selfish interests and emotions and the cultivation of more 'altruistic' or social sentiments" in the patient.[12]

Psychiatric Treatment in the 19th Century

Kraeplin provides further proof of these practices. He notes that toward the middle of the 19th century, doctors outdid themselves in "writing outlandish prescriptions, mainly for the reason that they tended to see a causal relation between their favorite influences and the resulting symptoms."[13] These prescriptions ranged from "pouring fifty to a hundred pails of ice-cold water on patients" to placing them on "whirling chairs capable of a hundred turns a minute." Emetics and purgatives were also very popular: "Emetics were supposed to convulse the patient and in this way to stimulate the nerves in the abdominal region and heighten the activity of various organs; to rid the stomach and upper enteron of mucus, bile, undigested food, poison, acids and other harmful substances; and finally, to calm or excite nerve centers antagonistically by inducing nausea."[14] Other treatment procedures included blood-letting to reduce excess blood in the brain, as well as the application of skin irritants that caused "blisters on the head and neck [and] were supposed to cause a transformation or 'metaschematism' of the disorder by checking perspiration, driving arthritis pain inward, and curdling milk."[15]

The epilogue to Kraeplin's book reveals the way psychiatry perceives its own progress. It shows how quickly psychiatry labels the treatments of the past as misguided or based on insufficient knowledge. Kraeplin wrote his history of psychiatry in 1917; however, its translation into English did not occur until 1962. Perhaps anxious to counter the negative impression with which the translation leaves the reader, an epilogue by psychiatrist Peter Laqueur follows the English edition. He begins by pointing out that "encouraging change has been taking place in the care of the mentally ill" since the time of Kraeplin and that "impressive advances have been made in the somatic treatment of psychiatric illness."[16] Laqueur goes on to list these "impressive advances":

᠅ Wagner-Jauregg's malarial treatment for general paresis (1917)
᠅ Manfred Sakel's insulin treatment for schizophrenia
᠅ Meduna's metrazol shock treatment (1928) and Cerletti and Bini's electric shock treatment (1938) for manic and depressive patients
᠅ The appearance of psychotropic drugs (1952)

ح Extensive use of prefrontal lobotomy (investigated by Kostic, 1953; in 1955 Egar Moniz won the Nobel Prize for his work in this field)[17]

A mere 50 years later, all of the above treatment categories — with the exception of the category of psychotropic drugs — have been declared by the psychiatric establishment as either ineffective, damaging, and/or dangerous. A textbook of psychiatry now calls the Wagner-Jauregg treatment of general paresis a blind alley of psychiatric research,[18] and the Sakel insulin treatment was deemed "unsatisfactory." Meduna, Cerletti, and Bini are barely mentioned, and the damaging effects of prefrontal lobotomy have been the subject of innumerable scientific studies, as well as the gruesome topic of popular books and films. The history of psychiatric treatment in recent decades reveals a disturbing picture of the purported efficacy and dangers of psychotropic drugs. It is sufficient to say that there exists ample historic and factual evidence for skepticism about psychiatry's present neuroscientific claims and its corresponding focus on physical treatments.

The Brain Disease Renaissance and
"The Decade of the Brain"

In 1990 President George Bush signed a congressional resolution that designated the 1990s as "The Decade of the Brain." To psychiatrist Peter Breggin, this was a campaign organized by the psychopharmacological industry, which is a trillion-dollar monopoly that funds psychiatric research, controls grant monies, and subsidizes most psychiatric conventions and many major psychiatric organizations. Its deep pockets even underwrite the American Psychiatric Association (APA). The interrelationship between psychiatry and the psychopharmaceutical industry originated in what has been called the drug revolution, which began in the 1950s when pharmaceutical companies developed (during the next 20 years) a series of new drug-categories: (1) neuroleptics (major tranquilizers),[19] (2) antidepressants, (3) lithium, and (4) benzodiazepines (minor tranquilizers such as Valium, and also those used in sleeping pills). Only a few decades earlier, the treatment of choice for the mentally distressed was the *talking cure* model.

A growing number of social critics, psychiatrists, and psychiatric hospital administrators have begun to criticize the pervasiveness of an exclusively biological paradigm for the treatment of mental illness. Tragically, it points to a wholesale resurgence of the 19th century conceptualization of mental illness as brain disease, one which could be effectively treated with drugs alone. Jerry Lewis, director of the psychiatric residency program at Timberlawn Psychiatric Hospital, bemoans the parochial view of present-day psychiatry. The pharmacological approach, by its nature, is single-symptom-focused. Yet, for Lewis, it is "painfully clear that all major psychiatric syndromes are heterogeneous."[20] Lewis describes psychiatry's current infatuation with biogenetic explanations of mental illness or distress as follows: "Psychiatry tends to advance on bandwagons, evangelical movements organized around a particular linear perspective on the etiology of major syndromes. Currently, the neuroscience bandwagon leads the parade; major syndromes are simply brain diseases; biological cures are around the corner; early development, psychodynamics, and social system variables, while interesting, are largely irrelevant."[21]

Psychiatry as Neuroscience

This heading captures the present-day climate in psychiatry, as well as that of the neuropsychological bandwagon of many of the non-medical psychotherapies. In a review of 1,236 articles of two major psychiatric journals within the span of 20 years, Pincus et al. found that "there is a continuing rise in the proportion of biologically oriented articles and also a drop in the proportion of psychologically and sociologically oriented articles, particularly those on psychological and behavioral precursors and mechanisms associated with particular mental disorders."[22] Melvin Sabshin points out that after the dominance of a pluralism of therapeutic approaches, American psychiatry in the past two decades retrenched into the domain of biology: "research in the neurosciences has advanced at a dizzying pace. While the advances have affected many medical specialties, the impact on psychiatry has been prodigious."[23]

Psychiatric training and education provides evidence of this influence. Major institutions such as Johns Hopkins Medical School have stopped requiring training in psychotherapy altogether for their psychiatric interns.[24] The search for meaning in the patient's symptoms, which was once an important part of American psychiatric training, even until the 1960s, has become a psychiatric subspecialty in which students, next to the ever increasing hours of required neuroscience training, can choose to minor. Few of the burgeoning classes of psychiatric interns elect a more holistic approach to mental health care. This is largely attributable to the fact that contemporary psychiatry views itself more and more as neuroscience. Psychiatrists, both in the United States and in Europe, seem increasingly enthusiastic about finding "genes that code for specific illnesses."[25] Breggin points out that the psychiatric residents he instructs "are very threatened by any suggestion that their patients suffer from psychosocial problems and that physical treatments might do more harm than good."[26]

How much psychiatry has changed within the last decades is echoed by the psychiatrist Marcio Vasconcellos Pinheiro, who received his psychiatric training in the United States in the early 1970s, before returning to his native Brazil. When he returned to America in the late 1980s, he wrote the following in the journal *Psychiatry*:

> *Since I returned to the United States, I have come across a whole new generation of psychiatrists, coming from the best medical schools, who are unable to pay attention to their patients' subjective worlds. They have been trained to look at peoples' outsides: behavior is what counts, in the best American, mechanistic, pragmatic tradition. In my opinion, American psychiatry, while considering itself more scientific, has returned to the unfortunate attitudes of pre-Freudian day. . . . My hope is that, sooner or later, the distortions I perceive will be corrected and priorities will again be set placing people as the main consideration.*[27]

Psychiatry has different priorities today. It wants to become as respected as medicine. When Herbert Pardes writes about educating psychiatrists, he cites as the number-one achievement that his profession has "once and for all established itself as part of medicine."[28] Not only does this accomplishment rank high on his list; it is an essential element to the resounding conclusion of his article which states: "I believe we will remember the decades from the mid-1980s into the 21st century as the time psychiatry came of age, was established as a solid and respected field within medicine, and dramatically augmented its ability to make a contribution to the alleviation of suffering."[29] Pardes's final remark about the alleviation of patients' suffering seems striking, for nowhere in this 10-page article that presents a version of a speech delivered to a meeting of the American Association of Directors of Psychiatric Residency Training does this phrase "alleviation of suffering," or even the word "suffering," appear. Analogously, in the 11 points that Pardes uses to summarize psychiatry's success story of the past decade, not one speaks to suffering, its mitigation, or makes reference to psychiatry having provided better care for patients. Instead, most of his statements point to the degree to which psychiatry has become increasingly recognized as a legitimate science. He cites the unprecedented funding for psychiatric research, the awards and accolades received, and the unprecedented influence of such governmental agencies as the National Institute for Mental Health (NIMH). The surest way to achieve such dubious legitimacy consisted of psychiatry's emphasis on its connection, not to psychotherapies, such as psychoanalysis, but to medicine.

Whereas the theory and praxis of psychotherapy — understood as non-pharmacological treatment of mental distress — constitutes a frequently ambiguous approach and one difficult to quantify in the vagaries of humane mental health care, biomedical procedures are supposed to be based on *hard* science.

The Doctor-Patient Relationship

The doctor/patient relationship enters into another aspect of psychopharmacological treatment best described as the symbolic meaning of the drug prescription. Balint uses the metaphor of the doctor-drug to characterize how a patient perceives the clinician's attitude when prescribing drugs. Rosin and Köhler have pointed out that psychiatrists might prescribe drugs rather than psychotherapy as a way of maintaining distance between themselves and their patients.[30] If this were the case, it would be an unfortunate situation wherein the caregivers are afraid to truly connect with persons seeking help, lest they risk the danger and vulnerability of establishing real relationships with them.

In their research, Rosin and Köhler emphasize the importance of understanding the psychodynamics between patient and psychiatrist. They believe that psychiatrists who understand the psychodynamic situation vis-à-vis their clients and reflect on the reasons behind their prescription of medication seem to be in the best position to provide optimal care for their patients.[31]

I emphasize the doctor/patient relationship because the psychopharmacological conception and approach to mental distress unknowingly relies in large measure on aspects of symbolic healing and the actual human contact the patient receives. The responsible prescription of drugs necessitates continuous follow-ups, consultations, and treatment reviews. Also, it requires the knowledge and willingness to implement non-pharmacological psychotherapeutics when indicated. In other words, drug therapy requires a certain sensitivity and empathy toward the patient, as well as time spent with them. Time, however, constitutes an especially scarce commodity in a system that places efficiency and productivity over human concerns. This is true of many aspects of American culture, of which psychiatry is as much a victim as are the patients. The present-day mental health arena "speaks the language of the New World Order: lean, efficient, productive, competitive, and guided by that last, living god, *The Market.*"[32] From the perspective of an economic bottom line, weekly therapy encounters seem inefficient. Much more desirable are once-a-month, 10-to-15-minute visits required for prescription renewal.

Conclusion

Power knows no bounds, and *much* wants more. Biopsychiatry's commitment to its singular view, propelled now by the marketplace, literally excludes the context of world.

This commitment dehumanizes and depersonalizes. What makes this narrow view especially troubling is the situation in which it occurs: suffering people in need of care, often shaken-up, anxious, emotionally unprotected, without outside support, lonely, isolated, and desperate, are entering the private office of a "healer." Many times these people possess only a small shred of hope that they will be able to exit their pain.

Present-day psychotherapeutics is not about helping as much as it is about maintaining the status quo. Carl Cohen has pointed out that the new psychiatry mirrors Western science's attempt to control and dominate our outer and inner nature, a control necessary as much for a capitalistic system intent on maximizing profits as for the continuation of social, professional, and political power structures.[1] The endless tale of patient abuses perpetrated by the psychiatric and the market establishment — of which only a few examples have been given here — provide abundant evidence of this observation.

Science and, more recently, economics justify these abuses based on rational, mathematical calculations of the bottom line. This approach has also been called *instrumental reason*,[2] which depends on the objective view of the subject. This view allows for the highest degree of efficiency and objectivity, and it is precisely efficiency and objectivity on which instrumental reason prides itself and regards as its outstanding achievement.[3]

Instrumental reason dominates reason and has become equated with reason itself. Focused on efficiency and objectification, instrumental reason represents a reason, which takes into account that "some must die" to achieve a practical end — be that in Tibet, Vietnam, Chile, Afghanistan, Nicaragua, Panama, or Iraq. It tries to dominate — be that one's own nature or someone outside of oneself.[4]

Instrumental reason fears the unknown, dreads imagination, and panics without icons. Suspicious of itself and its own origins, instrumental reason limits itself to controlled observations, experiments, and manipulation. Fearful of any deviance from the self-imposed structure, it is not satisfied until it has totalized its dominion, until other forms of thinking and being have been excluded. Instrumental reason does not allow any other gods next to itself.

But unlike the God who demanded, "Thou shalt not make unto thee any graven image . . . of anything that is in heaven above,"[5] the technical approach to human problems thrives on its own iconization. It reifies its past achievements throughout the modern cultural landscapes on plaques and statues, through industries and institutions, and in hospitals and psychiatric wards. It is intoxicated by an epistemological hubris, or presumption of knowledge, by what the German psychotherapist and social critic Richter once termed the *God-complex*.[6] It was precisely this hubris that Freud wanted to shatter, when almost a century ago, he proclaimed that we were not masters of our own house.

Instrumental reason has come to embody the way we think about healing. Recent appeals by some leading figures in American psychiatry and psychology attest to this fact.[7] Testimonials of many health care providers about the reality of present managed care show how thinking about profits seems all too often at odds with providing what these practitioners would deem good-quality care. This conflict is due largely to the fact that profit thinking is based on calculative reason whereas quality of care is grounded in a reason that eludes the former.

In the spirit of instrumental reason, the power in health care decision and policy making has been taken away from providers and placed into the hands of bureaucrats.[8] Hence, the question becomes how people can begin to stop this power drain and re-assert their humanity. As Margaret Mead points out in her inspiring and often quoted encouragement for challenging the status quo: "Never mind that a small group of thoughtful, committed citizens can change the world. Indeed, it is the only thing that ever has."[9]

So it seems to me now that those who understand the ongoing dehumanization process through bureaucratization (i.e., the government of instrumental reason); the trivialization of suffering through its decontextualization and professional transformation; and the degree to which money and power in the hands of individuals, organizations, and corporations shape the way we conceive of human beings and the way we care for them, must continue to make their voices heard. This implies the translation of understanding through the realm of the *polis*, through political action, certainly. Other loci of change can be found within psychotherapeutics and psychiatry themselves, whether in the therapy office, graduate training programs, or even conversations we share over lunch in break rooms.

Change also happens from those enraged enough from their own experience of being dehumanized to rally for something better. Examples abound of organizations small and large that have collectively created community around the experience of being pathologized, overmedicated, and dehumanized by the mental health care system. One powerful example is a community called the Icarus Project, a group founded by two people diagnosed with bipolar disorder who found the mental health system's definition of their experience to be narrow and stifling of their creative gifts.[10] As a result, they founded a community that has a presence in several U.S. cities and provides a safe space for individuals to explore their "mad gifts" together. The Icarus Project is just one example and hopefully a sign of a larger counter-movement standing up for a more humanistic view of human beings and their care.

Epilogue:
Toward a New Understanding
of Psychotherapeutics

Recognizing the questionable efficacy of psychotropic medications, and the dualistic underpinnings used to warrant their unilateral use in mental health, where do we turn? In other words, if the myth of a biochemical imbalance can no longer be supported as the underlying cause of mental duress, does there exist a set of guiding principles that enable clinicians to more fully encounter and *see* the person in need?

Returning to Heidegger and the notion of being-in-the-world, the field of psychotherapeutics cannot ignore the understanding garnered in the last century from the many disciplines ranging from literature to philosophy to theoretical physics. Such understanding requires clinicians to take into account the insights gained from this perspective. As a way of synthesizing my critique of medical model thinking and my argument for a being-in-the-world conceptualization of human suffering, I will present a number of concrete directions that may serve to guide a new generation of clinicians in the fields of psychiatry and psychotherapeutics.

Openness and Honesty

We live in a new era with a different mind-set, sensibility, and awareness. Clients who visit a psychiatrist or psychotherapist have changed. They no longer believe in the expert telling them what to do or how to behave. Instead, they seek partners who are open and honest about their own processes, their own humanity.

My personal breakthrough in therapy occurred when I walked into my therapist's office and saw her, full of anger, shout into the phone at her car mechanic who had not kept a promise he made about delivering her car on time. This led to many months of work on my own anger, which I had not expressed, and also pierced the idea that being a healthy person meant being beyond such strong emotions. Her showing me her real side, though unwittingly, made a big difference in my maturation process.

Interrelated with the World

Aside from therapists being transparent and real with their feelings, the new awareness longs for an understanding of human beings' interrelatedness with the world. We are not isolated beings but, using Heidegger's concept, beings-in-the-world who cannot be separated from the world in which we live.

Living in the world means that what happens in the world — wars, pollution, conflicts, celebrations — all affect me, often in overt but many times in subtle, imperceptible ways. I remember sitting in my therapist's office one time when the fire alarm in the building went off. He proceeded to sit there as if nothing had happened while the noise level of people shouting in the corridor grew louder and louder. Such stark differentiation between what is outside and inside belongs to an antiquated era of thought.

The Belief in Knowledge

Nietzsche famously posits that the biggest fable of all is the fable of knowledge[1] in a dictum that speaks to a mind-set more prevalent in the 21st century than it has ever been before. We have become suspicious of people stating they *know*, that they can say something definitively. We have witnessed a dramatic increase in viewpoints, and the concept of paradigm has become a household word. It is clear to many that knowledge is not fixed but depends on the background of the person or institution proclaiming it. Through the scientific revolutions of the last century, from a Newtonian to an Einsteinian and now toward a quantum physics paradigm, we have radically different frameworks for understanding the world.

In addition, through the breaking down of national borders and the process of globalization, we are increasingly aware of different spiritual and psychological traditions in the world, all basing their knowledge on different premises and assumptions. Eastern and Western approaches to understanding people and the planet now exist side by side in universities and other places of learning. In short, the concept of some form of static knowledge existing today — a knowledge that could be seen as a compass or divining rod — is regarded with increasing suspicion.

Living in the Question

The suspicion of knowledge being able to provide us with answers moves us to a different approach to life and living, one that the poet Rilke called "living in the question."[2] Our clients come to us with an expectation of receiving answers to their struggles, sufferings, and questions. This very attitude often lies at the heart of the problem that compels clients to enter the therapist's office.

Their desire to know and to have answers drives them to suffering when those answers simply cannot be given to them, or to anybody else for that matter. How should I answer the question: Shall I stay in this relationship with my wife/my husband? The question asked by my client points to the issue this client needs to face: I want answers to questions that can only be found by going through the process of learning and discovery, through staying in relationship with the issue that I face. Here, the desire for an answer constitutes the very source of suffering and the issue that needs to be addressed.

From Certainty to Uncertainty

Living in the question also means that we move toward understanding that life, fundamentally, is uncertain and cannot provide the kind of security that such certainty might hold for our clients. Here the question arises: What is good about certainty and makes it more desirable than uncertainty? Though certainty might give us the feeling that we know what will happen the next day and in the distant future, uncertainty can also be seen as providing us with the excitement of the unexpected, the unknown. Uncertainty lies at the heart of play, something we humans, as well as many animals, cherish and enjoy.

Clients who are distressed because of the lack of certainty in their lives enter the office of the psychotherapist with the hope that he or she can provide this certainty. The dominant mind-set supports the desire for certainty through many forms of insurances; through social, national, and retirement securities; and through many protections given to person and property. The existence of drugs that address specific psychic disturbances constitutes a form of reassurance and misplaced faith that the expert doctor knows the cure. But these protections and securities are mostly valid for the material world and speak little to the security our subjective reality feels in the world. This reality has different parameters and requires an attitude grounded in fluidity and unpredictability rather than fixed expectations.

Often, it is when these securities fall through that a person seeks out therapy. Trauma confronts us with the uncertain nature of reality, leaving us yearning for certainty, but perhaps needing balance instead.

This also speaks most directly to the ambiguity of suffering and further to the ambiguity of living. We help clients experience abject terror, followed by courage, confidence, and safety, then back to abject terror, then back to courage. In this way, clients become more comfortable in both qualities of living, as well as the processes in between.

Doing and Being

In the latter half of the 20th century, more and more voices could be heard emphasizing how many of us had become victims of the industrial production machine. We identified with the work we were doing and felt satisfaction only through what we achieved in the material world. Such an attitude that emphasizes *doing* over *being* led many people wanting to opt out of a society that was driven to produce at any cost. Concepts such as *rat race, workaholism,* and *workload* are descriptors for a tendency to value doing over being.[3]

Becoming aware of the mainstream-informed drive for doing and achieving, of identifying with what one does rather than who one is, can help clients become more clear and open about their often hidden hopes and desires. It is important that therapists do not signal in any way that they themselves prefer one way of being over another, so that clients are not afraid of being judged negatively if their lives lead them along the path less traveled, so to speak.

Therapists' openness and impartiality toward clients living their lives in any way they need to live is crucial for authentic becoming. For this to occur, therapists need to be aware of their own assumptions of what they conceive to be a life well lived. Do they feel supportive of a *being* stance that does not produce in the conventionally accepted sense? Do they have ideas of what form of success is most admirable? These are important questions for clinicians to ponder and cultivate awareness around.

Diagnosis and Process-Oriented Awareness Work

Diagnosis is an important feature of conventional psychotherapy and psychiatry. Such labeling is also popular because of its ability to quickly identify and categorize. However, this approach does not allow much room for the complexity and richness of the individual's purpose and history of symptoms and the world context within which they occur. Accessing such richness requires a deep curiosity and understanding of the meaning and process behind an individual's symptoms. Such meaning can unfold by allowing clients to enter into the world of their symptoms. Such immersion can allow clients to understand the possible function and purpose of their suffering. Instead of polarizing their suffering as a *bad* phenomenon, they may actually befriend their symptoms.

From a process-oriented point of view there exists no static label for a person's condition, only awareness of a momentary flow. Such an attitude understands therapy as awareness work rather than a treatment of suffering or pathology. Process orientation thus regards people's psychic and physical distress as a door through which to enter into an understanding of a person's life and direction. Such direction changes from moment to moment while a more fundamental pattern, also called the person's myth, remains.

From Content to Process

Traditional psychotherapy places much weight on the content of clients' verbal expressions. Of cour*se,* this is important for understanding clients' worlds and self-constructs, their history, and the issues with which they are struggling. However, the last century has revealed the way words and their meanings are not linked in any fixed way, but instead change with each person and with time. This insight changes the way we are with clients and how we work with them.

First, we pay as much attention to the nonverbal ways in which clients express themselves as to what is being said.

Second, we ask questions about the meaning of clients' utterances and words: What do you mean by this? What do you understand this word to mean? Act it. Sing it. Describe it. Pretend this word did not exist: How would you say it then? The signifier, the word, only *points* to the signified, the content of the word. The relationship between signifier and signified is tentative, imprecise, and ever-changing. Often this relationship serves more to obfuscate than to illuminate issues that a person faces.

Asking about the meaning that clients ascribe to the usage of their words is one way to be attentive, in general, to the complexity of language and, more specifically, to the complexity of clients' symptoms.

Holding the Paradox

Life is inherently paradoxical. We are born to die. Our life oscillates between highs and lows, between the polarities of pain and joy, darkness and light. One polarity is needed to give the other meaning. The word "paradox" derives from the Greek *paradoxos,* from "para," meaning on one side, beyond, and "doxa," meaning opinion. Thus, paradox literally means on the other side of an existing opinion.

We humans have a tendency to adhere to one side or the other and often need help to hold both parts of an opinion at the same time. This is what we call holding the paradox. Here we are referring to the fact that clients will invariably want to polarize their own as well as other peoples' lives and search outside themselves for the problem as well as the solution.

Concretely, clients often find themselves in the role of the victim, because it is they who are experiencing the suffering. It is an arduous process to help clients understand that in the end it is more complex than placing the perpetrator outside of themselves, that they themselves hold a certain responsibility to whatever has *happened* to them as well. Especially in relationship counseling, this can been witnessed more easily as both partners try to come to terms with the reality that the very person they love also inflicts pain and suffering.

Here, maturation occurs when clients understand not only that both realities co-exist, but that they themselves are able to give love as well as cause hurt. Here, clients move beyond the victim role to understanding how they partake in creating the reality in which they live. It is also a view that understands the interrelated and connectedness of all beings, a place beyond the duality of good and bad, right and wrong.

The Clinician as Human Being

The traditional model of psychotherapy understands the therapist as expert, someone who holds secret knowledge about life and living. The 21st century understanding of human beings as beings-in-the-world understands our interconnectedness in the way that it is our shared humanity that allows us to be present for each other and to know each other. This understanding has far-reaching implications for how therapists present themselves within their offices. Rather than the aloof expert, or the blank screen, therapists reveal their humanity and show their emotions as they relate to and encounter their clients. Therapists model how to be aware of who they are in the many moments of life. This awareness is reflected by therapists showing that they are human beings with feelings, by demonstrating openness to being challenged, and even welcoming the possibility of being wrong.

In this way they model the many facets of being human, from awareness to unawareness, from happiness to sadness, from openness to being closed.

Not-Knowing: Toward Curiosity and Play

Thinking in the 21st century has gone beyond the idea that there exists a static knowledge that can be used as a compass to navigate how we are to live our lives. What is required instead is an attitude of curiosity and play. Therapists can be the curious agents who challenge their clients to explore and discover on their own while learning that life is fluid and flows in many directions at the same time.

The element of play has been recognized by many sages over the period of recorded human history as the element that makes us quintessentially human. Play is the very human quality of loosening our entrapment in one or the other polarity. The element of play allows our intellectual mind — which desires to control outcomes and is driven by goals — to rest and relax, allowing for poignancy and joy.

Listening and *Listening*

The very foundation of any helping profession is listening to the person in need of help. Over the years, this need for true listening persists. That we cannot take for granted that each practitioner is in command of this basic, and yet central, skill has led various theoreticians and teachers to specify more closely what they feel listening entails. Listening was thus called active listening to emphasize that this is not an automatic act but one that requires an active stance on the side of the practitioner. It has also been called deep listening to stress that we listen to more than just the words but also to the many other subtleties of human communication.

These subtleties relate especially to nonverbal communication, the way the body speaks. But these subtleties also extend to how we feel in the room together with our clients, how we subjectively experience them, and what it is we sense. These ways of listening are often inaccessible to us but can greatly influence how we perceive clients in the room.

From Control to Mystery

We live in a world that provokes a craving for certainty, justifiably so. Such craving leads us to control our world maximally. We do not like to be surprised by the unknown, except when at play, in comedy, or with games. Our desire for control has led modern-day humans to contrive predictability in the world in which they live: transportation schedules; fixed open and closing times for stores, businesses, and work; and regular health check-ups, to name but a few. Living in such a world, it is relatively easy to forget the fragility of the system we have established — and how much of our lives are really out-of-control.

Moreover, thinking we have controlled our outer world, we often take our inner world for granted. Yet, both our inner and outer worlds remain deeply mysterious if we take a step back and exit the illusion of control and safety. We all know stories where suddenly another reality breaks in and reminds us of the unpredictability of life and that any one of us can be affected by unexpected changes to our lives. This reminder is important in our work with clients, because we want to stay open to the unpredictable, to what many writers have called the mystery of life.

Openness to mystery allows us to stay curious and know that there is always more to understand. To remember the mysterious quality of life also keeps our attitude humble when it comes to knowing the other. Such an attitude allows us to stay open to the constant flux of life.

The Method as Symptom

Clients who go to see a therapist reveal their suffering not only through the way they express their symptoms, but also in the way they desire to have their suffering addressed. This speaks to the method they deem appropriate to handle their concerns. For example, do clients want their therapist to solve their issues for them? Do they want to have their issues resolved quickly or do they have patience for the process to unfold? Does a client seek an emotional or rational solution to his or her issue? Are clients able to connect with their therapists? Are they able to trust and relate to them? What are the expectations with which the client enters the therapeutic process?

All these different methods add to therapists' appreciation for the complex nature of clients' many different forms of suffering and help to guide the therapeutic process forward. These methods also emphasize therapists' basic humanity and continued struggle for awareness and understanding — that they are an intimate part of all of the journeys we call life.

CƐ

Notes

Introduction

1. Shunryu Suzuki, *Zen Mind, Beginner's Mind* (Boston: Shambhala, 2006).
2. Carlos Castaneda, *The Teachings of Don Juan: A Yaqui Way of Knowledge* (New York: Penguin, 1968).
3. James Hillman, *The Dream and the Underworld* (New York: Harper & Row, 1979), 115.

Chapter 1

1. Hypnosis, in its early days, also known as magnetism or mesmerism, bases itself on the research of Franz Anton Mesmer in the early part of the 19th century. Henri F. Ellenberger, in *The Discovery of the Unconscious* (New York: Basic Books, 1970), gives a detailed account of the emergence of mesmerism in his chapter on "The Emergence of Dynamic Psychiatry," 53-109.
2. Quotations from Sigmund Freud from *The Standard Edition of the Complete Psychological Works of Sigmund Freud*, James Strachey, Ed. & Trans. (1900; London: Hogarth Press, 1953), are cited in the Notes with the abbreviation SE followed by volume and page numbers. Here: Sigmund Freud and Josef Breuer, "Studies on Hysteria," *SE*, 2: 185.
3. Freud quotes Meynert here in his "Review of Forel," *SE*, 1: 92.
4. Strachey remarks in his introduction to Freud's papers on hypnotism and suggestion (SE, 1: 64) that this visit to Paris had a "profound effect" on him as far as his acceptance of hypnosis was concerned. After his return from Paris, Freud gave two lectures on hypnotism before the Vienna Physiological Club and the Psychiatric Society, attesting further to how serious he took this therapeutic method. Even though Freud later abandoned hypnosis in his practice and theory — he felt that he was not very good at it clinically — Freud did give hypnosis much credit for the development of psychoanalytic theory. Strachey quotes two passages in which Freud expresses his

gratitude to hypnosis: "We must still be grateful to the old hypnotic technique for having brought before us single psychical processes of analysis in an isolated or schematic form. Only this could have given us the courage ourselves to create more complicated situations in the analytic treatment and to keep them clear before us" (SE, 12: 148 [1914]). And in 1916-17, in the Introductory Lectures: "We psychoanalysts may claim to be [hypnosis's] legitimate heirs and we do not forget how much encouragement and theoretical clarification we owe to it" (SE, 16: 462).

5.   Freud expressed in various contexts his fondness for basic research in the biological sciences. Had it not been for the need to earn a living for his family, he states at one point, he would have preferred research over the clinical work that was going to bring him the fame for which he so much longed in his younger years.

6.   But see also S. Bernfeld, "Freud's Earliest Theories and the School of Helmholtz," *Psychoanalytic Quarterly*, 13 (1944): 34–362, and his "Sigmund Freud, M.D., 1882–1885," *International Journal of Psycho-Analytics*, 32 (1951): 204.

7.   Robert R. Holt, "A Review of Some of Freud's Biological Assumptions and Their Influence on His Theories," in *Psychoanalysis and Current Biological Thought*, Norman S. Greenfield and William C. Lewis, Eds. (Madison: University of Wisconsin Press, 1965), 109.

8.   Peter Amacher, "Freud's Neurological Education and Its Influence on Psychoanalytic Theory," *Psychological Issues*, 4(4) (1965): 1-125.

9.   See Amacher, 21.

10. This understanding follows closely the philosophies of Locke, Berkeley, Hume, and Mill. An excerpt from Meynert's writings explains more clearly how he understands this passive spectator model: "Let us imagine the cortex to be a tabula rasa, and let us present it a phenomenon which, perceived by two different sensory surfaces, would, through the mediation of the corona radiata, stimulate two distinct areas of the cerebral cortex. Let the phenomenon in question be a lamb, and let us suppose that it emits a bleating sound. The sight of the lamb will stimulate cells in the auditory sphere. The lamb disappears and the two kinds of images which it caused to be registered will grow fainter. If, in the course of time, one of these registered images be revived, through the bleating, say of the lamb hidden in the stable, then not only the auditory, but the visual image also of the lamb will be reproduced. In the cortex an inference is made from the sound to the body that gave forth the sound. We can readily understand this process of induction, if we will assume that the original excitation of both sensory areas included the excitation of those arciform bundles which united the cells

of the visual and auditory areas the cortex, which areas in turn received stimulating impulses through the projection-bundles. In this way both registered images are associated, and whenever the one of them is re-excited, the excitation will extend along the association-fibres to the other cells, which on a previous occasion had been taken out of a condition of repose simultaneously with the cells harboring the former image. The association-bundles may be compared to a connecting thread, which enables one image to lift the other, as it were, over the threshold of consciousness. Inferring one attribute of a phenomenon from the presentation of another attribute, constitutes an induction; it is a recognition in the direction of causality, for the bleating sound is taken to be the result of the presence of the lamb." "Psychiatry," B. Sachs, Trans. (1884; New York: G. P. Putnam's Sons, 1885); quoted in Amacher, 27.

11. Amacher, 41.

12. Amacher, 50ff.

13. Sigmund Exner, *Entwurf zu einer physiologischen Erklärung der psychischen Erscheinungen* (Vienna, 1894); quoted in Amacher, 52.

14. In the preface to Bernheim's book on hypnosis, *Die Suggestion und ihre Heilwirkung*, Freud expresses the hope that "[o]nce the existence of objective, physiological phenomena in hysteria has been demonstrated, there is no longer any need to abandon the possibility that hysterical 'major' hypnotism may present phenomena which are not derived from suggestion on the part of the investigator" (*SE*, 1: 79).

15. Amacher points out that Freud published a number of articles on neurology as well as two volumes on clinical neurology. He also wrote on aphasia and cerebral paralyses (1897).

16. "Some Points for a Comparative Study of Organic and Hysterical Motor Paralyses," *SE*, 1: 161.

17. Sigmund Freud and Josef Breuer, "Studies on Hysteria," SE, 2: 185.

18. Freud did not title this work, even though he referred to it once as a "Psychology for Neurologists." The German edition, *Aus den Anfängen der Psychoanalyse* (From the beginnings of psycho-analysis), gave it the title *Entwurf einer Psychologie* (Sketch of a psychology). The Standard Edition refers to it as the *Project for a Scientific Psychology*.

19. Ernest Jones, *The Life and Work of Sigmund Freud, Vol. 1* (New York: Basic Books, 1953), 383.

20. Freud's letter to Fliess, May 25, 1895, SE, 1: 283.

21. Ernest Jones, in his chapter on "Freud's Theory of the Mind," allocates almost half of the 40 pages to a description of the Project. In his account of its contents, Jones notes that "all except the last three [of the list] were developed further in Freud's later writings, often thirty years later." The

list he gives is as follows: "Principles of Inertia and Constancy, Primary and Secondary Process, Unconscious and Preconscious, Urge towards Wish-Fulfillment, Hallucinatory and real fulfillment of Wishes, Criteria of Reality, Inhibitory function of the ego-Mobile and bound energy, Separation of function between perception and memory, Relation of Memory to contact barriers and facilitations, Three conditions for the arising of consciousness, Significance of Speech, Thought as experimental small-scale action, Traumas and pain as excessive stimuli, Protective screen against them and concentration of cathexes to deal with irruptions, No screen against internal stimuli, Signals of unpleasure instead of full doses, Dreams: wishful, hallucinatory, regressive, distorted — No motility during sleep, Parallelism of dreams and neurotic symptoms, Importance of sexuality in neuroses, Hysteria: defense, repression, displacement, distortion, Significance of Attention, Analysis of intellectual processes, including logical errors, etc., Connection between repression and retardation of puberty" (392).

22. See also Note 27. The *Project* was published in English in 1950 and in German in 1962.

23. *SE*, 1: 290 (editor's Introduction). See also Jones's biography, Chapter XIII.

24. Ernest Jones writes that Freud "shared this illusion [of brain physiology making order of the 'chaos of mental processes'] himself for many years, until there was a gradual liberation from it which was complete by 1897" (1: 379).

25. *SE*, 2: 185.

26. *SE*, 1: 290. Strachey's footnote is relevant here: "The curious student may follow this lengthy trail more particularly through the letters to Fliess of January 1 and December 6, 1896, Chapter VII of *The Interpretation of Dreams* (1900a), 'The Two Principles of Mental Functioning' (1911b), the metapsychological papers of 1915, *Beyond the Pleasure Principle* (1920g), *The Ego and the Id* (1923b), the 'Mystic Writing Pad' (1925a) and, finally, the *Outline of Psychoanalysis* (1940a) (1938)."

27. Jones writes that "we may regard the feverish writing of the Project as a last desperate effort to cling to the safety of cerebral anatomy" (384).

28. Jones, 384.

29. Freud envisages quantity as a fluid that moves in a complex hydraulic system.

30. Freud abbreviates external quantity as Q and internal, endogenous quantity as Qh.

31. Following standard anatomy of his time, Freud divides the nervous system into two functions: "the reception of stimuli from outside and the discharge of excitations of endogenous origin" (*SE*, 1: 297).

32. An idea Freud already introduced some months earlier in the "Studies on Hysteria."

33. Amacher, 68.

34. Jones writes that "we may regard the feverish writing of the Project as a last desperate effort to cling to the safety of cerebral anatomy" (384).

35. *SE*, 1: 290. Strachey's footnote is relevant here: "The curious student may follow this lengthy trail more particularly through the letters to Fliess of January 1 and December 6, 1896, Chapter VII of *The Interpretation of Dreams* (1900a), 'The Two Principles of Mental Functioning' (1911b), the metapsychological papers of 1915, *Beyond the Pleasure Principle* (1920g), *The Ego and the Id* (1923b), the 'Mystic Writing Pad' (1925a) and, finally, the *Outline of Psychoanalysis* (1940a) (1938)."

36. *SE*, 1: 295.

37. Jones, 384.

38. Freud envisages quantity as a fluid that moves in a complex hydraulic system.

39. Following standard anatomy of his time, Freud divides the nervous system into two functions: "the reception of stimuli from outside and the discharge of excitations of endogenous origin" (*SE*, 1: 297).

40. *SE*, 1: 297.

41. *SE*, 4: xxxii. Written in the preface to the 3rd (revised) English edition (March 15, 1931).

42. The structural model does not differ substantially from the topographic model. It represents, rather, a further refinement of Freud's topography, with the most significant change being the introduction of the ego-ideal or super-ego. Whereas in the early years Freud saw the ego as the agent that repressed the unconscious id-impulses, he began to understand in his work on narcissism that an ideal associated with the ego — the ego-ideal — and not the ego itself, was responsible for censorship and moral conscience. In *The Ego and the Id* (1923), his last major theoretical work, this ego-ideal evolved into what we now know as the super-ego. With the super-ego, Freud established the final tripartite division of id, ego, and super-ego. It was this tripartite psychic economy that comprised the standard terminology in all of his subsequent writings. Leading up to this final model were ideas outlined in the *Project*, *The Interpretation of Dreams*, and in the metapsychological writings of 1915. The Id, a term borrowed from Georg Grodeck's book titled *The Book of the It* (1923), connotes what Freud hitherto had referred to as the unconscious. The

change in terminology does not represent any conceptual departure. The ego continued to arbitrate the demands of the superego and the id. Its principal function was to inhibit the free-flowing "primary process" and is itself responsible for the control of the secondary process.

43. Jung, not caught in Freud's biological net, saw dreams rather as possessing a compensatory function. To him they were also "dress-rehearsals" for future modes of being and behaving. Dreams in Jung's view are therefore much more future oriented and are "progressive" to use Freud's language.

44. *SE*, 1: 318.

45. Freud's numerous publications on this subject, even after his experiences with Charcot and his own use of hypnosis, provide compelling evidence of his continuing ties to scientific orthodoxy.

46. *SE*, 1: 318. Strachey pointed out that Freud's description of the experience of satisfaction "is repeated very closely in Chapter VII of *The Interpretation of Dreams*, and again, though more shortly, in the paper on the two principles of mental functioning."

47. *SE*, 1: 319. Strachey noted that this idea surfaces again 20 years later in a metapsychological paper on dreams (there it is called the principle of the unsusceptibility to excitation of uncathected systems) in *Beyond the Pleasure Principle* (1920), and in the "Mystic Writing Pad" (1925).

48. Frank J. Sulloway, Freud, *Biologist of the Mind* (New York: Basic Books, 1979), 123.

49. Quoted in Sulloway, Freud, *Biologist of the Mind*, 124. Freud's letter is dated August 6, 1895, a time when he was in the middle of his research on the *Project*.

50. *SE*, 4: xv (editor's Introduction).

51. *SE*, 5: 511.

52. Holt wrote that Freud "did not attain methodological clarity about the nature and status of the nonneurological theory he ostensibly was building, particularly vis-à-vis the mind-body problem" (101).

Chapter 2

1. Letter to Fliess, October 15, 1897, in Jeffrey M. Masson, *The Complete Letters of Sigmund Freud to Wilhelm Fliess, 1887-1904* (Cambridge, MA: Belknap Press of Harvard University Press, 1985), 272.
2. *SE*, 4: 261.
3. *SE*, 4: 261–262.
4. *SE*, 4: 264.
5. *SE*, 4: 262.
6. *SE*, 4: 262.
7. Peter L. Rudnytsky, *Freud and Oedipus* (New York: Columbia University Press, 1987), 355.
8. Rudnytsky, 355.
9. The German passage, in Martin Heidegger's "Brief über den Humanismus" (1946), reads: "Sie fragen: Comment redonner un sens au mot »Humanisme«? Diese Frage kommt aus der Absicht, das Wort »Humanismus« festzuhalten. Ich frage mich, ob das nötig ist. Oder ist das Unheil, das alle Titel dieser Art anrichten, noch nicht offenkundig genug?" (Heidegger, Wegmarken, 313). The publication date points to the fact that Beaufret asked this question within the context of post–World War II.
10. *SE*, 4: 262.
11. Quoted by Freud (*SE*, 4: 263).
12. *SE*, 4: 264.
13. By then the Oedipus complex had, as Freud states in a footnote to the 1914 edition of *The Interpretation of Dreams*, thrown "a light of undreamt-of importance on the history of the human race and the evolution of religion and morality." It is, of course, quite amazing that Freud omits over half of his listeners in the audience, that is, the female population.
14. *SE*, 16: 331.
15. *SE*, 16: 331.
16. *SE*, 13: 156.
17. Pietro Pucci, *Oedipus and the Fabrication of the Father* (Baltimore, MD: Johns Hopkins University Press, 1992).
18. Pucci, 9.
19. Pucci, 9.
20. Unless otherwise indicated, translations are by Robert Fagles, *The Three Theban Plays* (New York: Penguin Classics, 1984), 1301.

21. Pucci states: "tukhê does not oppose the notion of divine fate but corroborates it, through emphasizing the aoristic aspect of the event rather than the perfective one of a set program" (12).

22. *SE*, 4: 262.

23. Jean Pierre Vernant and Pierre Vidal-Naquet, *Myth and Tragedy in Ancient Greece* (New York: Zone Books, 1990), 93. Following quotations from the same source are referenced in the Notes with MT for the title abbreviation followed by page numbers.

24. *MT*, 88.

25. *MT*, 89–90.

26. Vernant thus calls the domain of tragedy "that border zone where human actions are intermeshed with divine powers and reveal their true meaning, unsuspected even by those who initiated them and bear responsibility for them, when they fall into place in an order which is beyond man himself and eludes him" (92).

27. See Note 26.

28. As Vernant puts it: "[T]he opposition between philia and eros, family attachment and sexual desire, holds a place of major importance in the structure of the drama. When the two are confused together and one called a 'substitute' for the other, the text is not made clearer; on the contrary, the play is ruined" (102).

29. It is beyond the scope of this work, but the question arises as to whether Freud's reading, then, could be about Sophocles, who does know all these things? Or the primordial author of the myth itself? Could Freud, perhaps even unconsciously, be speaking of them and how the play reveals that they participate in this unconscious, albeit forbidden desire?

30. *MT*, 105.

31. *MT*, 105.

32. *MT*, 105.

33. *MT*, 105.

34. *MT*, 109.

35. P. Vidal-Naquet, "Oedipus in Athens," in Vernant and Vidal-Naquet, 326.

36. Martha Nussbaum, *The Fragility of Goodness* (Cambridge, UK: Cambridge University Press, 1986), 26.

37. Nussbaum, 26.

38. Nussbaum, 51.

39. Nussbaum, 51.

40. Rainer Maria Rilke, *Lyrik und Prosa*, Käte Hamburger, Ed. (Frankfurt: Insel Verlag, 1977).

41. The Declaration of Independence, of course, is a document shaped at the height of the 18th-century Enlightenment.

42. Rollo May, "The Meaning of the Oedipus Myth," *Review of Existential Psychiatry and Psychology, 1* (1961): 48.

43. That morality is not something given but created is Merleau-Ponty's definition of morality. Merleau-Ponty is a representative of existential-phenomenological philosophy and someone who applied his philosophical insights increasingly to questions of modern psychology toward the end of his life.

44. May, 50.

45. *Oedipus at Colonus*, lns. 312–314. Sophocles, *The Three Theban Plays: Antigone, Oedipus the King, Oedipus at Colonus*, Robert Fagles, Ed. (New York: Penguin Classics, 1984).

46. *Oedipus at Colonus*, lns. 641–651.

47. *Oedipus at Colonus*, ln. 670.

48. *Oedipus at Colonus*, lns. 1096–1098.

49. *Oedipus at Colonus*, lns. 1884–1887.

49. *Oedipus at Colonus*, lns. 1887–1891.

50. *Oedipus at Colonus*, lns. 1999–2001.

51. *Oedipus at Colonus*, lns. 1999–2001.

52. Martin Heidegger, "Nachwort zu: 'Was ist Metaphysik?'" in Wegmarken, 310: "Doch laßt nun ab, und nie mehr fürderhin Die Klage wecket auf; Überallhin nämlich hält bei sich das Ereignete verwahrt ein Entscheid der Vollendung." The English translation by Richard Wiseman is titled *Therapies of Literature: How Long Has It Been Since the Future?* (2003). I am indebted to Dr. Wiseman for helping me clarify Heidegger's intention in translating Sophocles in this particular way.

53. "That much I know, now that I hear the oracles my dear one brings and brood on the old prophecies, stored in the depths of all my being, that Apollo has fulfilled for me at last" (Pucci, 507–511).

54. James Hillman, *Revisioning Psychology* (New York: Harper & Row, 1975), 74.

55. *SE*, 22: 211.

56. "That much I know, now that I hear the oracles my dear one brings and brood on the old prophecies, stored in the depths of all my being, that Apollo has fulfilled for me at last" (Pucci, 507–511).

57. I am indebted to James Hillman's lecture "Oedipus Revisited" given at the Eranos Conference in Ascona, Switzerland, in 1987. It was originally published by Crossroad. Rudolf Ritsema, Ed., *Eranos Yearbook 56–1987* (Frankfurt: Insel Verlag, 1989), 261–307. The lecture also appears in *Oedipus Variations: Studies in Literature and Psychoanalysis* (Dallas: Spring, 1991), 89–169. I quote from the latter publication.

58. Erich Fromm has written a very pertinent essay to this issue titled "The Oedipus Complex: Comments on the Case of Little Hans" (in The Crisis of Psychoanalysis [New York: Henry Holt, 1991]). Fromm points out how Freud, in his analysis of little Hans, is guided again and again by the presupposition of the existence of the Oedipus complex. This bias leads Freud to ask suggestive questions and make suggestive interpretations. Fromm cites the following exchange between Freud and little Hans as an example. Freud plays Hans's father in this conversation: Father: "Then why do you always cry whenever Mummy gives me a kiss? It's because you are jealous?" Hans: "Jealous, yes." Father: "You'd like to be Daddy yourself." Hans: "Oh, yes." Father: "What would you like to do if you were Daddy?" Hans: "And you were Hans? I'd like to take you to Linz every Sunday — no, every week-day too. If I were Daddy I'd be ever so nice and good." Father: "But what would you like to do with Mummy?" Hans: "Take her to Linz, too." Father: "And what besides?" Hans: "Nothing." Father: "Then why are you jealous?" Hans: "I don't know." And later, Father: "Did you often get into bed with Mummy at Gmunden?" Hans: "Yes." Father: "And you used to think to yourself you were Daddy?" Hans: "Yes." Father: "And then you felt afraid of Daddy?" Hans: "You know everything; I didn't know anything." Father: "When Fritzl fell down you thought: 'If only Daddy would fall down like that!' And when the lamb butted you, you thought: 'If only it would butt Daddy!' Can you remember the funeral at Gmunden?" Hans: "Yes. What about it?" Father: "You thought then that if only Daddy were to die you'd be Daddy." Hans: "Yes" (97-98). It is difficult to ascertain what are Hans's spontaneous responses and what are responses to Freud's suggestive questions and interpretations.
59. Fromm, 135.
60. *Oedipus Tyrannus*, lns. 75-79. Sophocles, The Three Theban Plays: Antigone, Oedipus the King, Oedipus at Colonus, Robert Fagles, Ed. (New York: Penguin Classics, 1984).
61. Hillman, "Oedipus Revisited," 107.
62. Hillman, "Oedipus Revisited," 122. This more psychological interpretation of the oracle may be "too modern." Perhaps the Greeks, given their own historicity, were not able to understand in this way.
63. *Oedipus Tyrannus*, lns. 1251-1253.
64. James Hillman, *Revisioning Psychology* (New York: Harper & Row, 1975), 74.
65. *Oedipus Tyrannus*, lns. 1831-1832.

Chapter 3

1. Heidegger's letter to Husserl, October 22, 1927; in Walter Biemel, *Heidegger* (Reinbek, Germany: Rowohlt Taschenbuch, 2002), p. 300.
2. See Note 1.
3. However, both Newton and Galileo, embedded within a religious worldview, still possessed a profound respect for the special place the human being held in the world of inanimate beings.
4. Subsequent quotations from Martin Heidegger, *Being and Time, John Macquarrie and Edward Robinson, Trans.* (New York: Harper & Row, 1962), are cited in the Notes with the abbreviation *BT* followed by the page number: *BT*, 32.
5. *BT*, 32.
6. "And because we cannot define Dasein's essence by citing a 'what' of the kind that pertains to a subject-matter, and because its essence lies rather in the fact that in each case it has its Being to be, and has it as its own, we have chosen to designate that entity 'Dasein,' a term which is purely an expression of its Being" (*BT*, 33).
7. *BT*, 33.
8. Martin Heidegger, *Existence and Being*, Werner Brock, Ed. (Chicago: Henry Regnery, 1949), 26.
9. As Brock points out, the Heideggerian world follows the Greek concept of *kosmos* as used, for example, by Parmenides, Heraclitus, and Anaxagoras.
10. *BT*, 177.
11. *BT*, 277.
12. *BT*, 434f.
13. *BT*, 435ff.
14. *BT*, 264.
15. This is also expressed in a fascinating passage by Thomas Mann in his essay on Schopenhauer. He writes: "The human being who has done a criminal deed, may have, as empirical character, acted in a necessary way and under the influence of certain motives, but he could have been different — and also the bite of conscience, the angst of conscience, is directed onto Being, not onto the act." And Mann follows with the comment: "What a courageous, a deeply felt and at the same time icy thought." (Der Mensch, der das Strafbare getan, hatte zwar notwendig, als empirischer Charakter, unter dem Einfluß bestimmter Motive, so gehandelt, aber er hätte können anders sei, — und auch der Gewissensbiß, die Gewissens-angst zielten aufs Sein, nicht auf

das Handeln. Kühner, tief gefühlter und dabei harter Gedanke!). See especially Thomas Mann's *Felix Krull.*

16. *BT*, 264.

17. *BT*, 50. Heidegger defines phenomenology more precisely as "to let that which shows itself be seen from itself in the very way in which it shows itself from itself" (58). This, states Heidegger, expresses no more than the Husserlian maxim "To the things themselves!" Heidegger gives a detailed analysis of the term phenomenology by going back to the meaning of the Greek words *phainómenon* and *lógos.* The word "phenomenon" itself, derived from the Greek *phainesthai*, connotes "to shine forth, unveil itself, come out of concealment or darkness" (see especially *BT*, 49–63).

18. Heidegger gives a brief introduction to the phenomenon of being-in before his discussion on the concept of world. He justifies this as follows: "The fact that we foresaw this structural item [being-in] which carries so much weight, arose from our aim of setting the analysis of single items, from the outset, within the frame of a steady preliminary view of the structural whole, and of guarding against any disruption or fragmentation of the unitary phenomenon" (*BT*, 169).

19. *BT*, 81.

20. A dog certainly is aware of being touched. The emphasis is on the experience of touch.

21. *BT*, 169.

22. René Descartes, *Meditations* (London: Penguin Classics, 1980), 102. The *Meditations* were first published in 1641. Further citations are cited in the Notes with the abbreviation *Med.* followed by the page number.

23. *Med.*, 102.

24. *Med.*, 105.

25. *Med.*, 105. Descartes does, toward the end of his argumentation, maintain that the body, from a practical, everyday standpoint, belongs to the thinking subject.

26. *Med.*, 132.

27. *Med.*, 156.

28. *Med.*, 150.

29. *Med.*, 156.

30. *BT*, 168f.

31. *BT*, 170.

32. *BT*, 94.

33. *BT*, 94 (translation mine).

34. Wilhelm Dilthey, to whom Heidegger expressed his indebtedness, has phrased this concisely as follows: "The special character of life is

understood by means of categories which do not apply to our knowledge of physical reality." *Pattern and Meaning in History* (New York: Harper & Brothers, 1962), 105.

35. *BT*, 105.
36. *BT*, 107.
37. Also his statement: "In anything ready-to-hand the world is already 'there,'" and "Along with Dasein as being-in-the-world, entities within-the-world have in each case already been disclosed" (*BT*, 114, 251).
38. *BT*, 149.
39. *BT*, 150. Whereas "ontic" refers to plain or observable facts, as those studied in biology or chemistry, "ontological" denotes those meaningful structures at an existential level, those in reference to Being itself.
40. *BT*, 150.
41. *BT*, 150.
42. His teacher Husserl, as many of his predecessors influenced by the Cartesian tradition, share the argument that the cogito is self-evident, that it is given and thus unambiguous. We become aware of our consciousness, says Husserl, through inner perception, through the subject bending and directing itself back to view itself. The logic of this reflexive model is based on spatial and visual metaphors borrowed from the outside world and then imposed onto the "inner" world. The validity of this transposition, however, is not necessarily given. This inner perception model cannot explain, for instance, the emergence of the phenomenon of self-consciousness itself. How do I know that I, the subject, am looking at my own self and not onto something else? I can only know that I am looking at myself if I have already some knowledge of myself. It would not be possible to know that I am looking at myself without possessing an awareness of myself first. I must, therefore, have a prior understanding of myself.
43. *BT*, 151.
44. *BT*, 151.
45. *BT*, 150.
46. *BT*, 150.
47. *BT*, 152.
48. Hurbert Dreyfus, in his commentary on *Being and Time* (*Being-in-the-World: A Commentary on Heidegger's* Being and Time (Cambridge, MA: MIT Press, 1991), specifically highlights this point. Referencing Wittgenstein, he writes: "It is important at this point to remember that Heidegger, like Wittgenstein, is not denying conscious experiences. Like Wittgenstein, he is trying to get rid of a certain picture of the self as containing a self-contained stream of experiences that are its essential

content. What Heidegger denies is the foundational significance of mental states. He points out that what is *'given' in reflection does not have the priority in everyday life that it has in Cartesian philosophy"* (147; italics mine).

49. *BT*, 153.
50. *BT*, 154f.
51. *BT*, 156.
52. As with the phenomenon of being-in, Heidegger foresees at this point the "structural item" of Care in order not to lose sight of the structural whole of Dasein. The way Dasein relates to other entities called Dasein is not in the way it relates to equipment or Things, but is in the way of Care (Fürsorge). Care is what Heidegger calls the Being of Dasein. We care in many different ways for our being and that of others. Care is therefore grounded in Dasein's fundamental characteristic of being-with and being with others. (See especially *BT*, 39–41.)
53. *BT*, 167.
54. *BT*, 167.
55. *BT*, 166.
56. *BT*, 165.
57. *BT*, 165.
58. With its strong allusion to biblical scripture, however, it is difficult to read the term in a neutral way.
59. *BT*, 312.
60. Søren Kierkegaard, in *Sickness unto Death* (Princeton, NJ: Princeton University Press, 1980), gives a very poignant description of people who have given up the challenge to be themselves: "Surrounded by hordes of men, absorbed in all sorts of secular matters, more and more shrewd about the ways of the world — such a person forgets himself, forgets his name divinely understood, does not dare to believe in himself, finds it too hazardous to be himself and far easier and safer to be like the others, to become a copy, a number, a mass man. . . . Because a man is in this kind of despair, he can very well live on in temporality, indeed, actually all the better, can appear to be a man, be publicly acclaimed, honored, and esteemed, be absorbed in all the temporal goals. . . . They use their capacities, amass money, carry on secular enterprises, calculate shrewdly, etc., perhaps make a name in history, but themselves they are not; spiritually speaking, they have no self, no self for whose sake they could venture everything, no self before God — however self-seeking they are otherwise" (34f).
61. *BT*, 169.

AMBIGUITY OF SUFFERING

62. "Mood" is the translation of *Befindlichkeit*. Heidegger derives this term from the German expression Wie befinden sie sich? This expression literally means "how one finds oneself," that is, in what mood one finds oneself or how one is currently attuned to oneself and the world.

63. *BT*, 173.

64. The English translators use "state of mind" rather than "mood" to capture the German term *Befindlichkeit* or *Stimmung*. A particular use of the word "mood" in English retains this notion of self-location. Aircraft, both in outer space and in the atmosphere, describe their position in terms of the aircraft's "mood." This "mood" is described in terms of pitch and yaw of the craft—the position of the nose versus that of the tail, the level or non-level posture of the vehicle, and so forth.

65. *BT*, 174.

66. *BT*, 177.

67. For a more detailed discussion of the concept of mood in Heidegger, see Bruce Ballard, The Role of Mood in Heidegger's Ontology (London: University Press of America, 1991).

68. *BT*, 264.

69. *BT*, 190.

70. *BT*, 194.

71. *BT*, 193.

72. *BT*, 204.

73. *BT*, 205.

74. *BT*, 205.

75. *BT*, 206.

76. *BT*, 208.

77. *BT*, 208.

78. *BT*, 152.

79. Heidegger states this as follows: "To have faith in the Reality of the 'external world,' whether rightly or wrongly; to 'prove' this Reality for it, whether adequately or inadequately; to pre-suppose it, whether explicitly or not — attempts such as these which have not mastered their own basis with full transparency, presuppose a subject which is proximally worldless or unsure of its world, and which must, at bottom, first assure itself of a world" (*BT*, 250).

80. "The 'scandal of philosophy' is not that this proof has yet to be given, but that such proofs are expected and attempted again and again. Such expectations, aims, and demands arise from an ontologically inadequate way of starting with something of such a character that independently of it and 'outside' of it a 'world' is to be proved as present-at-hand. . . . If Dasein is understood correctly, it defies such proofs, because,

in its Being, it already is what subsequent proofs deem necessary to demonstrate for it" (*BT*, 249).

81. *BT*, 247.
82. *BT*, 251.
83. *BT*, 254.
84. *BT*, 254.
85. *BT*, 249. It is because of this fall that Dasein "loses its ability to see" the fact of its worldliness and can regard the world as objects present-at-hand, separate from itself: "In falling, Dasein itself as factical Being-in-the-world, is something from which it has already fallen away. And it has not fallen into some entity which it comes upon for the first time in the course of its Being, or even one which it has not come upon at all; it has fallen into the world, which itself belongs to Dasein" (220).
86. Heidegger comments on the circular structure of understanding as follows: "[A]ccording to the most elementary rules of logic, this circle is a circulus vitiosus. . . . But if we see this circle as a vicious one and look for ways of avoiding it, even if we just 'sense' it as an inevitable imperfection, then the act of understanding has been misunderstood from the ground up. . . . The 'circle' in understanding belongs to the structure of meaning, and the latter phenomenon is rooted in the existential constitution of Dasein — that is, in the understanding which interprets. An entity for which, as Being-in-the-world, its Being is itself an issue, has, ontologically, a circular structure" (*BT*, 194f).
87. *BT*, 246, 215.
88. It is precisely Heidegger's point that "[b]y this priority the route to a genuine existential analytic of Dasein gets diverted, and so does our view of the Being of what is proximally ready-to-hand within-the-world. It finally forces the general problematic of Being into a direction that lies off course. The other modes of Being become defined negatively and privatively with regard to Reality" (*BT*, 245). Heidegger is careful to point out, though, that the present-at-hand understanding of the human being has its own purposes and advantages. It becomes problematic, however, if it is the preferred, prioritized way of understanding the human being. For a more comprehensive discussion of these arguments, see also Dreyfus's commentary Being-in-the-World, especially Chapter 15.

Chapter 4

1. Melvin Konner, *Medicine at the Crossroads: The Crisis in Health Care* (New York: Pantheon Books, 1993).
2. Konner, 160,
3. Konner, 160.
4. Konner, 160f.
5. *Oedipus at Colonus*, lns. 2000–2001.
6. *Oedipus at Colonus*, lns. 649–651.
7. Greek pathos, related to *páshkein* (suffer) and *pénthos* (grief).
8. *Oxford English Dictionary* (1989).
9. *Oxford English Dictionary* (1989).
10. Most of modern pathology is based on autopsies, performed in numbers as early as the 16th century.
11. *Oxford English Dictionary* (1989).
12. S. L. Robbins, R. S. Cotran, and V. Kumar, *Pathologic Basis of Disease* (Philadelphia: W. B. Saunders, 1984), 1.
13. E. F. Gilbert and R. W. Huntington III, *An Introduction to Pathology* (Oxford, UK: Oxford University Press, 1978), 5.
14. Disease is contrasted to illness, which is "personalized and refers to disease in a specific patient." J. B. Wyngaarden and L. H. Smith, Eds., *Textbook of Medicine* (Philadelphia: W. B. Saunders, 1988), 71. The distinction between suffering and illness is more difficult to make. Both suffering and illness are personal: I suffer, I am ill (versus I have a disease). I can be ill but need not necessarily suffer — as is true of the converse. The link between suffering and illness exists insofar as I experience myself as being ill, just as in suffering I am normally aware of my suffering. The difference between suffering and illness lies perhaps more in the knowledge of etiology. An illness has frequently a more defined or determined origin, many times linked to a singular "cause," whereas in suffering the etiology is often not clearly defined or unknown. Furthermore, suffering is seldom of a singular origin but rather connected to a multiplicity of reasons and concerns.
15. *New Encyclopaedia Britannica*, Vol. 17 (1990), 313. "The 'normal' or 'physiologic' state is achieved by adaptive responses to the ebb and flow of various stimuli permitting the cells and tissues to adapt and to live in harmony within their microenvironment. Thus, homeostasis is preserved." Robbins et al., 1.

16. Robbins et al., 1.
17. For the physician or physiologist, suffering is often a sign of an "out-of-control" illness, an illness that has resisted and continues to resist standard medical treatment, lies beyond the clinician's repertoire, knowledge, or treatment skill. In the West, a patient's condition of suffering often points to the very limitations of just this medicine.
18. Eric Cassell, "The Nature of Suffering and the Goals of Medicine," *New England Journal of Medicine*, 306 (1982): 639–645. Cassell published a book by the same title.
19. Cassell, 639.
20. Compare the passion of Christ, perhaps the only remaining expression in English retaining the original meaning.
21. Greek pathos, related to *páshkein* (suffer) and *pénthos* (grief). Merriam-Webster (2013), from the ancient Greek.
22. Karl Baier, "Gesundheit, Krankheit, und Genesung," *Daseinsanalyse*, 9 (1992): 285–306. In the following exposition I am indebted to Baier's astute analysis of the interrelation between illness and world.
23. Baier.
24. Baier.
25. *BT*, 167.
26. *BT*, 166.
27. In German those who suffer with the ill person are called *Mitleidende*, literally, "those who suffer with."
28. Baier.
29. Leo Tolstoy, *The Death of Ivan Illych and Other Stories* (New York: Barnes & Noble, 2004), 137.
30. Alice Holzhey-Kunz, "Die Zweideutigkeit seelischen Leidens," Daseinsanalyse, 5 (1988): 81–95.
31. See Hans-Georg Gadamer, *Truth and Method*, Joel Weinsheimer and Donald G. Marshall, Trans. (New York: Crossroad, 1992), 295f, 358f. Gadamer restates Heidegger's *man* (they-self) as our belonging to tradition. For Gadamer our primordial understanding of world, our fore-knowledge and fore-conceptions, rely on the ground that tradition provides.
32. Breuer and Freud, in "Über den psychischen Mechanismus hysterischer Phänomene" (1893), had stated that hysterics was suffering from reminiscences, from a psychic fixation to (an) event(s) in childhood.
33. Holzhey-Kunz, 86.
34. Holzhey-Kunz, 86.
35. Holzhey-Kunz, 86.
36. Rollo May, *The Courage to Create* (New York: W. W. Norton, 1994), 76.

37. "Der Philosoph zieht sein Interesse vom konkret Alltäglichen ab, um sich auf seine Sache konzentrieren zu können, während der seelisch Leidende vom Alltäglichen selbst unfreiwillig auf die philosophische Dimension verwiesen wird, nicht dank philosophischer Besinnung auf die menschlichen Grundfragen, sondern im »Erleiden« ontologischer Wahrheiten; jede alltägliche Erfahrung stösst den Leidenden auf Grenzen — und lässt ihn anstossen" (Holzhey-Kunz, 92f).

38. Rainer Maria Rilke, *Lyrik* und *Prosa*, Käte Hamburger, Ed. (Frankfurt: Insel Verlag, 1975), 463. "Wir Vergeuder der Schmerzen. Wie wir sie absehn voraus, in die traurige Dauer, ob sie nicht enden vielleicht. Sie aber sind ja unser winterwähriges Laub, unser dunkeles Sinngrün, eine der Zeiten des heimlichen Jahres, — nicht nur Zeit, — sind Stelle, Siedlung, Lager, Boden, Wohnort" (*Duineser Elegien*, excerpt from the 10th elegy).

39. Friedrich Nietzsche, *Ecce Homo* (Munich: Goldmann, 1972): "Die Krankheit brachte mich erst zur Vernunft" (102), and "[Die Krankheit] beschenkte mich mit der Nötigung zum Stillegen, zum Müßigang, zum Warten und Geduldigsein. . . . Aber das heißt ja denken!" (140).

40. Alice Holzhey-Kunz, "Der Wunsch — daseinsanalytisch wiederentdeckt," *Daseinsanalyse*, 4 (1987): 63.

41. See works by A. Koestler, *The Act of Creation* (1975); A. Storr, *The Dynamics of Creation* (1976); G. Becker, *The Mad Genius* (1978); A. Rothenberg, *The Creative Goddess: The Creative Process in Art, Science, and Other Fields* (1979); T. Amabile, *The Social Psychology of Creativity* (1983); D. K. Simonton, *Scientific Genius* (1988); and A. Rothenberg, *Creativity and Madness* (1990).

42. G. R. DeLong and A. Aldershof, "Associations of Special Abilities with Juvenile Manic-Depressive Illness," *Annals of Neurology*, 14 (1983): 362.

43. R. L. Richards, D. K. Kinney, I. Kunde, and M. Benet, "Creativity in Manic-Depressives, Cyclothymes, and Their Normal First–Degree Relatives: A Preliminary Report," *Journal of Abnormal Psychology*, 97 (1988): 281–288.

44. A. M. Ludwig, "Creative Achievement and Psychopathology," *American Journal of Psychotherapy*, 46(3) (July 1992): 330–356.

45. Ludwig, 349.

46. Ludwig, 350.

47. Ludwig, 351.

48. Ludwig, 352.

49. Kay R. Jamison, "Mood Disorders and Patterns of Creativity in British Writers and Artists," *Psychiatry*, 52 (May 1989): 125-134.

50. Jamison, 125.

51. Whereas in the general population, "rates for bipolar and unipolar disorder are 1% to 5%," the research sample showed an affliction rate of 38%.

52. Jamison lists the results of other studies corroborating his findings, most notably Andreasen's research with the University of Iowa Writer's Workshop, where "80% of a sample of 30 writers had experienced an episode of affective illness."

53. Jamison, 131.

54. Jamison, 132.

55. F. Baron, "The Psychology of Imagination," *Scientific American* (September 1958); quoted in Larry Dossey, Space, *Time and Medicine* (Berkeley, CA: Shambhala, 1982), 85.

56. Medard Boss, *Psychoanalysis and Daseinsanalysis* (New York: Basic Books, 1963), 5.

57. Boss, 5.

58. Boss, 5.

59. Boss, 5.

60. Boss, 12.

61. Boss, 13.

62. Boss, 20.

63. The use of art therapy was very much a part of this case. The patient had drawn and painted many pictures before, which the therapist used in his work with her.

64. Boss, 22.

65. See Ludwig Binswanger, "The Case of Ellen West," in *Existence: A New Dimension in Psychiatry and Psychology*, Rollo May, Ed. (New York: Simon & Schuster, 1958). There, the patient is caught in the order of her own world (Eigenwelt), unable to change because of her fear of disorder. She longs for nothing more than to escape her own prison, an escape — or so she thinks — only possible through her death. Death for Ellen West belonged to her own order or sense of self.

66. J. A. Talbott, R. E. Hales, and S. C. Yudofsky, Eds., *Textbook of Psychiatry* (Washington, DC: American Psychiatric Press, 1988), 163. Diagnosis (from the Greek *diagignoskein* — to distinguish) is "the art of identifying a disease from its signs and symptoms" (one of Webster's definitions of diagnosis).

67. Karl Menninger, "The Psychiatric Diagnosis," *Bull Menninger Clinic*, 23 (1959): 226–240; quoted in R. E. Kendell, "Uses and Abuses of Diagnosis," in *Divergent Views in Psychiatry*, M. Dongler and E. D. Wittkower, Eds. (New York: Harper & Row, 1981), 5.

68. R. E. Kendell's book, *The Role of Diagnosis in Psychiatry* (Oxford, UK: Blackwell, 1975), was considered a basic reference.

69. Kendell, "Uses and Abuses of Diagnosis," 8.

70. Kendell, "Uses and Abuses of Diagnosis," 8.

71. Kendell, "Uses and Abuses of Diagnosis," 8. Kendell quotes a colleague here.

72. Kendell, "Uses and Abuses of Diagnosis," 8.

73. Friedrich Nietzsche, *Will to Power*, Walter Kaufmann and R. J. Hollingdale, Trans., Walter Kaufmann, Ed. (New York: Random House, 1968), 301.

74. T. S. Eliot, *Chorus from the Rock* (New York: Harcourt Brace Jovanovich, 1964).

75. Definition of *diagnosis* in Encyclopaedia Britannica: http://www.britannica.com/EBchecked/topic/161063/diagnosis/24607/Historical-aspects. Retrieved 2013.

76. Kendell, "Uses and Abuses of Diagnosis," 13.

77. Kendell, "Uses and Abuses of Diagnosis," 13. These studies were conducted in the 1950s and included both psychologists and psychiatrists.

78. Kendell, "Uses and Abuses of Diagnosis," 20.

79. Arthur Kleinman, *Re-thinking Psychiatry: From Cultural Category to Personal Experience* (New York: Free Press, 1991), 3.

80. Kleinman, 12.

81. Kleinman, 61.

82. Kleinman, 66.

83. Karl Menninger, "Changing Concepts of Disease," *Annals of Internal Medicine*, 29 (1948): 318–325.

Chapter 5

1. I emphasize theoretical foundation because, in praxis, many health care professionals will develop their own approach to therapeutic diagnostics and intervention often markedly deviating from their learning after leaving their educational and training institutions. Yalom remarked this fact in his book *Existential Psychotherapy* (New York: Basis Books, 1980), 21–23.

2. This is in itself a complex issue. Besides the shaping that occurs through theoretical training influenced by certain philosophical stances and beliefs, much of the history of therapeutics has been tool and

institutionally driven. Technologies such as microscopes, surgical tools, X-rays, pharmaceuticals, and today's CT scans have greatly influenced medical and therapeutic procedures. At the same time, educational and training institutions, as well as professional organizations, hospitals, and test labs have assured a certain consistency and quality of training.

3.   I understand empathy as defined by Book: "a spontaneous, intrapsychic, preconscious, and temporary experience occurring within the therapist, having affective/cognitive components whereby this therapist comes to know and comprehend what the patient might be experiencing consciously, preconsciously, or unconsciously." Along with Jaffe, Book further defines empathy as the therapist's ability "to think with the patient affectively, and then also to think about the patient — or perhaps more accurately to think about thinking with that patient. . . . Quite important, the capacity for empathy is an essential prerequisite for our ability to 'be empathic': to voice our empathic understanding of the patient's inner world in such a way that the patient feels understood and soothed." H. Book, "Is Empathy Cost Efficient?" *American Journal of Psychotherapy*, 45(1) (January 1987): 25.

4.   K. N. Lohr, Ed., *Medicare: A Strategy for Quality Assurance, Vol. 1* (Washington, DC: Institute of Medicine; National Academy Press, 1990); quoted in Lisa I. Iezzoni, "Monitoring Quality of Care: What Do We Need to Know?" *Inquiry*, 30 (Summer 1993): 112.

5.   The literature on the history of psychiatry and the role of physical treatments within this history is too abundant as to be referenced here. The reader is referred to additional works whose references have been the subject of extensive reviews, for instance, Bernhard Pauleikhoff's two volumes titled *Das Menschenbild im Wandel der Zeit: Ideengeschichte der Psychiatrie und Psychologie* (Hürtgenwald, Germany: Guido Pressler Verlag, 1983), written in German; additional studies by Andrew T. Scull, especially his *Desperate Remedies: A Social History of Somatic Treatments for Mental Illness* (Oxford, UK: Polity Press, 1988), and *Social Order/Mental Order* (Berkeley: University of California Press, 1989); Robert Castel, *The Regulation of Madness* (Oxford, UK: Polity Press, 1988); and Vieda Skultans, Ed., *Madness and Morals: Ideas on Insanity in the Nineteenth-Century* (London: Routledge & Kegan Paul, 1975). For an excellent study on German psychiatry in the 19th century, see Gerlof Verwey, *Psychiatry in an Anthropological and Biomedical Context: Philosophical Presuppositions and Implications of German Psychiatry, 1820–1870* (Dordrecht, Netherlands: D. Reidel, 1985). For a description of French psychiatry in the last century, see Jane Goldstein, *Console and Classify:*

The French Psychiatric Profession in the Nineteenth Century (Cambridge, UK: Cambridge University Press, 1987).

6. Emil Kraeplin, *One Hundred Years of Psychiatry* (New York: Philosophical Library, 1962); and Andrew T. Scull, *Museums of Madness* (London: Penguin Books, 1979).

7. Scull.

8. Scull, 148.

9. Scull, 165. Scull quotes here from the *Journal of Mental Science* (October 2, 1858).

10. Michael Clark, "The Rejection of Psychological Approaches to Mental Disorder in Late Nineteenth-Century British Psychiatry," in Madhouses, Mad-Doctors and Madmen: The Social History of Psychiatry in the Victorian Era, A. Scull, Ed. (Philadelphia: University of Pennsylvania Press, 1981), 271.

11. Clark, 276.

12. In Andrew Scull, Ed., *Madhouses, Mad-Doctors and Madmen: The Social History of Psychiatry in the Victorian Era* (Philadelphia: University of Pennsylvania Press, 1981), 300–301. For a more specific treatment on the political issues in the history of psychiatry in the United States, see also Kathleen Jones, *Mental Health and Social Policy, 1845–1959* (London: Routledge & Kegan Paul, 1960).

13. Kraeplin, 56.

14. Kraeplin, 58f.

15. Kraeplin, 61.

16. Kraeplin, 157f.

17. Kraeplin, 158.

18. Harold I. Kaplan and Benjamin J. Sadock, Eds., *Comprehensive Textbook of Psychiatry* (Baltimore: Williams & Wilkins, 1989), 640.

19. Neuroleptics are also referred to as major tranquilizers, antipsychotics, or ataraxics. The following drug classifications are included: phenothiazines, dibenzazepines, diphenylbutylpiperidines, thioxanthenes, butyrophenones, rauwolfia, and indolones.

20. Jerry M. Lewis, "Systems, Stress, and Survival: Psychiatric Hospitals in the 1990s," *Psychiatric Hospital*, 22(4) (1991): 147.

21. Lewis, 147.

22. H. A. Pincus, B. Henderson, D. Blackwood, and T. Dial, "Trends in Research in Two General Psychiatric Journals in 1969–1990: Research on Research," *American Journal of Psychiatry*, 150 (January 1, 1993): 141.

23. Melvin Sabshin, "Turning Points in American Psychiatry," *American Journal of Psychiatry*, 147 (October 10, 1990): 1271.

24. Kaplan and Sadock, 640.

25. Peter R. Breggin, *Toxic Psychiatry* (New York: St. Martin's Press, 1991), 14.
26. Breggin, 14.
27. Marcio V. Pinheiro, "Psychiatry"; quoted in Breggin, 16.
28. Herbert Pardes, "Educating Psychiatrists for the 1990s," *Academic Psychiatry*, 13(1) (Spring 1989): 3. Pardes's emphasis on incorporating psychiatry into medicine has subsequently been rewarded. The January 21, 1994, issue of Psychiatric News reports the following: "The voice of psychiatry will be a little more prominent in the house of medicine with the recent naming of Herbert Pardes, M.D., as chairman elect of the Council of Deans of the Association of American Medical Colleges."
29. Pardes, 12.
30. U. Rosin and G. K. Köhler, "Psychodynamic Aspects of Psychopharmacology in Functional Somatic Complaints," *Psychotherapy and Psychosomatics*, 56 (1991): 129–134. This holds especially true if the clinician feels imposed upon by the patient.
31. Rosin and Köhler.
32. Matthew P. Dumont, "The Privatization of Mental Health Services: The Invisible Hand at Our Throats," *American Journal of Orthopsychiatry*, 62(3) (July 1992): 328.

Conclusion

1. Carl I. Cohen, "The Bio-Medicalization of Psychiatry: A Critical Overview," *Community Mental Health Journal*, 29(6) (December 1993): 509–521.
2. There exists quite a varied literature on this subject. Besides Heidegger (*What Is Called Thinking; The Question of Technology*) and the Frankfurt School (Dialectic of Enlightenment, and Instrumental Reason [Horkheimer]), there are also current social critics writing on the danger and consequences of instrumental reason. For instance, W. Barrett, *Irrational Man, and The Illusion of Technique*; and T. Roszak, *Where the Wasteland Ends*.
3. What I mean to refer to is the fact that instrumentality has its place and is important as an approach (e.g., as in having your appendix removed). Again, the stress is on the exclusivity that the calculative approach demands for itself. For instance, in the case of fatigue, a frequent medical complaint, whose most common etiology is not physiological in origin, the practitioner's first response is, nevertheless, to treat the

condition as a biologically based syndrome. Rarely are social or other factors considered.

4. See Theodor W. Adorno and Max Horkheimer, *Die Dialektik der Aufklärung* (Frankfurt: Fischer Verlag, 1982), 1–41.

5. Exodus 20:4–6.

6. Horst-Eberhard Richter, *All Mighty: A Study of the God Complex in Western Man.* (Claremont, CA: Hunter House, 1984).

7. In an address to his professional colleagues, psychiatrist and congressman James McDermott phrases the issue facing contemporary psychotherapeutics as follows: "The fundamental question that needs to be simply put is this: Does the doctor-patient relationship mean anything at all in the human healing process? If your answer is a resounding yes, my next question is, What are you going to do to stop the erosion of the touchstone of medicine?" For McDermott the doctor-patient relationship lies at the core of healing and expresses itself foremost in the practitioner's ability to hear the client. But he warns that this capacity to listen has been seriously endangered through managed care. He quotes health economist Uwe Reinhardt in saying that five years from now all doctors will be "serfs of the insurance industry." *Psychiatric News,* June 17, 1994, 2/22. Psychiatrist Jerry Wiener strikes a similar tone in his appeal "to move beyond reductionism" and "encompass our diversity, based first on what is best for the patient and second based on mutual respect for each other." Wiener laments the increased tendency toward the corporate ownership of hospitals whose values are driven more by the pursuit of profit than quality of care. *Psychiatric News,* June 17, 1994, 22.

8. James A. Morone has argued this point eloquently in "The Health Care Bureaucracy: Small Changes, Big Consequences," *Journal of Health Politics, Policy and Law,* 18(3) (Fall 1993): 724. He finds that the "emerging American health politics increasingly operates with the language, methodology, and mind-set of bureaucratic actors."

9. Attributed to Margaret Mead. In Frank G. Sommers and Tana Dineen, *Curing Nuclear Madness: A New-Age Prescription for Personal Action* (London: Methuen, 1984), 158.

10. See www.theicarusproject.net, a project co-founded by Sascha DeBrul and Jacks McNamara. Their mission states: "We are a network of people living with and/or affected by experiences that are commonly diagnosis and labeled as psychiatric conditions. We believe these experiences are mad gifts needing cultivation and care, rather than diseases or disorders. By joining together as individuals and as a community, the intertwined

threads of madness, creativity, and collaboration can inspire hope and transformation in an oppressive and damaged world. Participation in The Icarus Project helps us overcome alienation and tap into the true potential that lies between brilliance and madness."

Epilogue

1. Martin Heidegger, *Nietzsche: Vol. III: The Will to Power as Knowledge and as Metaphysics*, and *Vol. IV*: Nihilism, David Farrell Krell, Ed. (San Francisco: HarperCollins, 1991), 555.
2. Rainer Maria Rilke, *Letters to a Young Poet*, M. D. Herter Norton, Trans. (rev. ed.) (New York: W. W. Norton, 1954).
3. See Erich Fromm, *The Art of Being* (1976).
4. See James Bugental, *Psychotherapy Isn't What You Think* (1999).

Bibliography

Abbey, S. E., & Garfinkel, P. E. (1991). Neurastenia and chronic fatigue syndrome: The role of culture in the making of a diagnosis. *American Journal of Psychiatry*, 148(12), 1638–1645.

Adorno, T. W., & Horkheimer, M. (1982). *Die Dialektik der Aufklärung.* Frankfurt: Fischer.

Amacher, P. (1965). Freud's neurological education and its influence on psychoanalytic theory. *Psychological Issues*, 4(4), 1–125.

Baier, K. (1992). Gesundheit, Krankheit, und Genesung. *Daseinsanalyse*, 9, 285–306.

Ballard, B. (1991). *The role of mood in Heidegger's ontology.* Boston: University Press of America.

Baron, F. (1958, September). The psychology of imagination. *Scientific American.*

Barrett, W. (1978). *The illusion of technique: A search for meaning in a technological civilization.* Garden City, NJ: Anchor Press.

———. (1978). *Irrational man: A study in existential philosophy.* Westport, CT: Greenwood Press.

Bateson, G. (1979). *Mind and nature: A necessary unity.* Toronto: Bantam Books.

Becker, G. (1978). *The mad genius controversy: A study in the sociology of deviance.* Beverly Hills, CA: Sage.

Bernfeld, S. (1944). Freud's earliest theories and the School of Helmholtz. *Psychoanalytic Quarterly*, 13, 341–362.

————. (1951). Sigmund Freud, M.D., 1882–1885. *International Journal of Psycho-Analytics, 32,* 204.

Bettelheim, B. (1991). *Freud's Vienna.* New York: Random House.

Binswanger, L. (1963). *Being-in-the-world.* New York: Basic Books.

Bizi-Nathaniel, S., Granek, M., & Golomb, M. (1991). Psychotherapy of an Arab patient by a Jewish therapist in Israel during the Intifada. *American Journal of Psychotherapy, 45*(4), 595–603.

Böhme, G. (1990). Sinn und Gegensinn — über die Dekonstruktion von Geschichten. *Psyche, 44*(7), 577–592.

Book, H. E. (1991). Is empathy cost efficient? *American Journal of Psychotherapy, 45*(1), 21–30.

Boss, M. (1975). *Es träumte mir vergangene Nacht . . .* Bern, Switzerland: Verlag Hans Huber.

————. (1975). *Grundriss der Medizin und der Psychologie.* Bern, Switzerland: Verlag Hans Huber.

————. (1976). *Indienfahrt eines Psychiaters.* Bern, Switzerland: Verlag Hans Huber.

Bouvard, M. P., & Mouren-Siméoni, M. C. (1990). La prescription des neuroleptiques chez l'enfant. *L'Encephale, 16,* 389–398.

Breggin, P. R. (1991). *Toxic psychiatry.* New York: St. Martin's Press.

Brenner, H. M. (1973). *Mental illness and the economy.* Cambridge, MA: Harvard University Press.

Breuer, J., & Freud, S. (1895). Studies on hysteria. In J. Strachey (Ed. & Trans.), *The standard edition of the complete psychological works of Sigmund Freud* (Vol. 2, pp. 1–335). London: Hogarth Press.

Brock, W. (Ed.). (1949). *Existence and being.* Chicago: Henry Regnery.

Brown, P., & Funk, S. C. (1986). Tardive dyskinesia: Barriers to the professional recognition of an eatrogenic disease. *Journal of Health and Social Behavior, 27,* 116–132.

Bugental, J.F.T. (1987). *The art of the psychotherapist.* New York: W. W. Norton.

Carucci, L. M. (1993). Medical magic and medicinal cure: Manipulating meanings with ease of disease. *Cultural Anthropology, 8*(2), 157–168.

Cassell, E. (1982). The nature of suffering and the goals of medicine. *New England Journal of Medicine*, 306, 639–645.

Castel, R. (1988). *The regulation of madness*. Cambridge, UK: Polity Press.

Chapman, S. (1979). Advertising and psychotropic drugs: The place of myth in ideological reproduction. *Social Science and Medicine*, 13A, 751–764.

Clark, M. (1981). The rejection of psychological approaches to mental disorder in late nineteenth-century British psychiatry. In Andrew Scull (Ed.), *Madhouses, mad-doctors and madmen: The social history of psychiatry in the Victorian Era* (pp. 271–312). Philadelphia: University of Pennsylvania Press.

Clinton, H. R. (1994). Meaningful health reform: The time is now. *Health Affairs*, Spring, 7–8.

Cohen, C. I. (1993). The bio-medicalization of psychiatry: A critical overview. *Community Mental Health Journal*, 29(6), 509–521.

———. (1993). Progressive psychiatry: A research agenda. *Community Mental Health Journal*, 29(6), 561–567.

Collins, H. M. (1993). The structure of knowledge. *Social Research*, 60(1), 95–101.

Condrau, G. (1977). *Der Januskopf des Fortschritts*. Bern, Switzerland: Bentelli Verlag.

Condrau, G. (1989). *Daseinsanalyse*. Freiburg, Germany: Universitätsverlag.

———. (1989). *Einführung in die psychotherapie*. Frankfurt: Fischer Verlag.

Csordas, T. J. (1993). Somatic modes of attention. *Cultural Anthropology*, 8(2), 135–156.

Delgado, A., Lopez-Fernandez, L. A., & Dios Luna, J. D. (1993). Influence of the doctor's gender in the satisfaction of the users. *Medical Care*, 31(9), 795–800.

DeLong, G. R., & Aldershof, A. (1983). Associations of special abilities with juvenile manic-depressive illness. *Annals of Neurology*, 14, 362.

Descartes, R. (1980). *Meditations*. London: Penguin Classics.

Dilthey, W. (1962). *Pattern and meaning in history*. New York: Cambridge University Press.

Dossey, L. (1982). *Space, time and medicine*. Berkeley, CA: Shambhala.

Dreyfus, H. (1991). *Being-in-the-world: A commentary on Heidegger's* Being and Time. Cambridge, MA: MIT Press.

———. (1993). Heidegger's critique of the Husserl/Searle account of intentionality. *Social Research*, 60(1), 17–38.

Drob, S. L. (1989). The dilemma of contemporary psychiatry. *American Journal of Psychotherapy*, 18(1), 54–67.

Dumont, M. (1990). In bed together at the market: Psychiatry and the psychopharmaceutical industry. *American Journal of Orthopsychiatry*, 60(4), 484–485.

———. (1990). Managed care, managed people, and community mental health. *American Journal of Orthopsychiatry*, 60(2), 166–167.

———. (1992). The privatization of mental health services: The invisible hand at our throats. *American Journal of Orthopsychiatry*, 62(3).

Eisenberg, L. (1986). Mindlessness and brainlessness in psychiatry. British *Journal of Psychiatry*, 148, 497–508.

Eliot, T. S. (1964). *Chorus from the rock*. San Diego: Harcourt Brace Jovanovich.

Ellenberger, H. F. (1970). *The discovery of the unconscious*. New York: Basic Books.

Engel, G. L. (1992). How much longer must medicine's science be bound by a seventeenth century world view? *Psychotherapy and Psychosomatics*, 57, 3–16.

Exner, S. (1894). *Entwurf zu einer physiologischen Erklärung der psychischen Erscheinungen*. Leipzig, Germany, & Vienna: Franz Deuticke.

Fagles, R. (1984). *The three Theban plays*. New York: Penguin Classics.

Fink, M. L. (1993). Managed care is not the answer. *Journal of Health Politics, Policy and Law*, 18(1), 105–112.

Frank, J. D. (1963). *Persuasion and healing*. New York: Schocken Books.

Frank, R., & McGuire, T. G. (1986). A review of studies of the impact of insurance on the demand and utilization of speciality mental health services. *Health Services Research*, 21(2), 241–265.

Freud, S. (1895). Project for a scientific discovery. In J. Strachey (Ed. & Trans.), *The standard edition of the complete psychological works of Sigmund Freud* (Vol. 1, pp. 283–387). London: Hogarth Press.

———. (1900). The interpretation of dreams. In J. Strachey (Ed. & Trans.), *The standard edition of the complete psychological works of Sigmund Freud* (Vols. 4 & 5, pp. 1–715). London: Hogarth Press.

———. (1920). Beyond the pleasure principle. In J. Strachey (Ed. & Trans.), *The standard edition of the complete psychological works of Sigmund Freud* (Vol. 18, pp. 7–64). London: Hogarth Press.

———. (1923). The id and the ego. In J. Strachey (Ed. & Trans.), *The standard edition of the complete psychological works of Sigmund Freud* (Vol. 19, pp. 12–66). London: Hogarth Press.

———. (1940). An outline of psycho-analysis. In J. Strachey (Ed. & Trans.), *The standard edition of the complete psychological works of Sigmund Freud* (Vol. 23, pp. 139–207). London, UK: Hogarth Press.

Fromm, E. (1991). *The crisis of psychoanalysis.* New York: Henry Holt.

Gabbard, G. O. (1992). The big chill: The transition from residency to managed care nightmare. *Academic Psychiatry*, 16(3), 119–126.

———. (1992). Psychodynamic psychiatry in the 'Decade of the Brain.' *American Journal of Psychiatry*, 149(8), 991–998.

Gadamer, H.-G. (1992). *Truth and method.* New York: Crossroad.

Gay, P. (1988). *A life for our time.* New York: W. W. Norton.

Gilbert, E. F., & Huntington III, R. W. (1978). *An introduction to pathology.* Oxford, UK: Oxford University Press.

Gilman, S. L. (1988). *Disease and representation: Images of illness from madness to AIDS.* Ithaca, NY: Cornell University Press.

Gitlin, M. J. (1990). *The psychotherapist's guide to psychopharmacology.* New York: Free Press.

Glaser, W. A. (1993). Universal health insurance that really works: Foreign lessons for the United States. *Journal of Health Politics, Policy and Law*, 18(3), 695–722.

Glazer, W. M., & Kane, J. M. (1992). Depot neuroleptic therapy: An underutilized treatment option. *Journal of Clinical Psychiatry*, 53(12), 426–433.

Goldstein, J. (1987). *Console and classify: The French psychiatric profession in the nineteenth century.* Cambridge, UK: Cambridge University Press.

Good, B. J. (1993). Culture, diagnosis and comorbidity. *Culture, Medicine and Psychiatry*, 16, 427–446.

Gregory, R. J., Jimerson, D. C., Walton, B., Daley, J., & Paulsen, R. H. (1992). Pharmacotherapy of depression in the medically ill: Directions for future research. *General Hospital Psychiatry*, 14, 36–42.

Hansen, T. E., Brown, W. L., Weigel, R. M., & Casey, D. E. (1992). Underrecognition of tardive dyskinesia and drug-induced parkinsonism by psychiatric residents. *General Hospital Psychiatry*, 14, 340–344.

Hawkins, A. H. (1992). Charting Dante: The Inferno and medical education. *Literature and Medicine*, 11(2), 200–215.

Heidegger, M. (1927/1962). *Being and time*. New York: Harper & Row.

———. (1929/1978). Nachwort zu: Was ist Metaphysik? In F.-W. von Herrmann (Ed.), *Wegmarken*. Frankfurt: Vittorio Klostermann.

———. (1946/1978). Brief über den humanismus. In F.-W. von Herrmann (Ed.), *Wegmarken*. Frankfurt: Vittorio Klostermann.

Herxheimer, A., Stålsby Lundborg, C., & Westerholm, B. (1993). Advertisements for medicines in leading medical journals in 18 countries: A 12-month survey of information content and standards. *International Journal of Health Services*, 23, 163–172.

Hillman, J. (1975). *Loose ends*. Dallas: Spring.

———. (1975). *Revisioning psychology*. New York: Harper & Row.

———. (1991). *Blue fire*. Thomas Moore (Ed.). New York: Harper Perennial.

———. (1991). *Oedipus variations: Studies in literature and psychoanalysis*, Dallas: Spring.

Hölderlin, F. (1989). Fragment von Hyperion. In *Hölderlin's Werke* (Vol. 2). Berlin & Weimar, Germany: Aufbau Verlag.

———. (1990). *Hyperion and selected poems*. New York: Continuum.

Holt, R. R. (1965). A Review of some of Freud's biological assumptions and their influence on his theories. In N. S. Greenfield & W. C. Lewis (Eds.), *Psychoanalysis and current biological thought* (pp. 93–124). Madison: University of Wisconsin Press.

Holzhey-Kunz, A. (1987). Der Wunsch — daseinsanalytisch wiederentdeckt. *Daseinsanalyse*, 4, 51–64.

———. (1988). Die Zweideutigkeit seelischen Leidens. *Daseinsanalyse*, 5, 81–95.

Hsia, D., & Ahern, C. A. (1992). Good quality care increases hospital profits under prospective payment. *Health Care Financing Review*, 13(3), 17–26.

Iezzoni, L. I. (1993). Monitoring quality of care: What do we need to know? *Inquiry*, 30, 112–114.

Jamison, K. R. (1989). Mood disorders and patterns of creativity in British writers and artists. *Psychiatry*, 52(2), 125–134.

Jellinek, M. S., & Nurcombe, B. (1993). Two wrongs don't make a right. *Journal of the American Medical Association*, 270(14), 1737–1739.

Johnstone, L. (1989). *Users and abusers of psychiatry*. London: Routledge.

Jones, E. (1953). *The life and work of Sigmund Freud, Vol. 1, 1856–1900*. New York: Basic Books.

Jones, K. (1960). *Mental health and social policy: 1845–1959*. London: Routledge & Kegan Paul.

Kaitin, K. I., Bryant, N. R., & Lasagna, L. (1993). The role of the research-based pharmaceutical industry in medical progress in the United States. *Journal of Clinical Pharmacology*, 33, 412–417.

Kane, J. M., & Smith, J. M. (1982). Tardive dyskinesia: Prevalence and risk factors, 1959 to 1979. *Archives of General Psychiatry*, 39, 473–481.

Kaplan, H. I., & Sadock, B. J. (Eds.). (1989). *Comprehensive textbook of psychiatry* (5th ed.). Baltimore: Williams & Wilkins.

Kendell, R. E. (1975). *The role of diagnosis in psychiatry*. Oxford, UK: Blackwell.

———. (1981). Uses and abuses of diagnosis. In M. Dongler & E. D. Wittkower (Eds.), *Divergent views in psychiatry*. New York: Harper & Row.

Kierkegaard, S. (1980). *The concept of anxiety: A simple psychologically orienting deliberation on the dogmatic issue of hereditary sin*. Princeton, NJ: Princeton University Press.

———. (1980). *The sickness unto death: A Christian psychological exposition for upbuilding and awakening*. Princeton, NJ: Princeton University Press.

Kleinman, A. (1991). *Re-thinking psychiatry: From cultural category to personal experience*. New York: Free Press.

Kleinman, A., & Kleinman, J. (1991). Suffering and its professional transformation: Toward an ethnography of interpersonal experience. *Culture, Medicine and Psychiatry*, 15(3), 275–301.

Kleinman, D. L., & Cohen, L. J. (1991). The decontextualization of mental illness: The portrayal of work in psychiatric drug advertisements. *Social Science and Medicine*, 32(8), 867–874.

Knowles, C. (1990). Afro Caribbeans and schizophrenia: How does psychiatry deal with issues of race, culture and ethnicity? *Journal of Social Policy*, 20(2), 173–190.

Koestler, A. (1964). *The act of creation.* London: Arkana.

Konner, M. (1993). *Medicine at the crossroads: The crisis in health care.* New York: Pantheon Books.

Koumjian, K. (1981). The use of Valium as a form of social con9trol. *Social Science and Medicine*, 15(3), 245–249.

Kraeplin, E. (1962). *One hundred years of psychiatry.* New York: Philosophical Library.

Lasch, C. (1979). *The culture of narcissism.* New York: Warner Books.

Lavin, M. R., & Rifkin, A. (1993). Diagnosis and pharmacotherapy of conduct disorder. *Progressive Neuro-Psychopharmacological and Biological Psychiatry*, 17(6), 875–885.

Lewis, J. (1991). Systems, stress, and survival: Psychiatric hospitals in the 1990s. *Psychiatric Hospital*, 22(4), 145–151.

Lexchin, J. (1988). The medical profession and the pharmaceutical industry: An unhealthy alliance. *International Journal of Health Services*, 18(4), 603–616.

———. (1989). Doctors and detailers: Therapeutic education or pharmaceutical promotion? International Journal of Health Services, 19(4), 663–679.

Lohr, K. N. (Ed.). (1990). *Medicare: A strategy for quality assurance* (Vol. 1). Washington, DC: Institute of Medicine; National Academy Press.

Ludwig, A. M. (1992). Creative achievement and psychopathology. *American Journal of Psychotherapy*, 46(3), 330–356.

Markowitz, J., Brown, R., Sweeney, J., & Mann, J. J. (1987). Reduced length and cost of hospital for major depressions in patients treated with ECT. *American Journal of Psychiatry*, 144, 1025–1029.

Marra, T. (1993). Prescription privileges offers improved access to care, reduced costs. *California Psychologist*, 26, 5.

Martin, E. (1993). Psychotropic and narcotic drugs and quality of life. In S. Streufert & F. Gengo (Eds.), *Effects of drugs on human functioning* (pp. 70–113). Basel, Switzerland: Karger Verlag.

Masson, J. M. (Ed. & Trans.). (1985). *The complete letters of Sigmund Freud to Wilhelm Fliess, 1887–1904*. Cambridge, MA: Belknap Press of Harvard University Press.

Maxmen, J. (1985). *The new psychiatry*. New York: William Morrow.

May, R. (Ed.). (1958). *Existence: A new dimension in psychiatry and psychology*. New York: Simon & Schuster.

———. (1961). The meaning of the Oedipus myth. *Review of Existential Psychiatry and Psychology*, 4(1), 22–36.

———. (Ed.). (1969). *Existential psychology*. New York: Random House.

———. (1979). *Psychology and the human dilemma*. New York: W. W. Norton.

McGuire, T. G. (1981). *Financing psychotherapy*. Cambridge, MA: Ballinger.

———. (1992). Research on economics and mental health: The past and future prospects. In R. G. Frank & W. G. Manning Jr. (Eds.), *Economics and mental health*. Baltimore: Johns Hopkins University Press.

McIntyre, J. (1994). Don't throw that couch out. *Psychiatric News*, 29, 3.

Meltzer, H. Y. (1992). Treatment of the neuroleptic-nonresponsive schizophrenic patient. *Schizophrenia Bulletin*, 18(3), 515–542.

Menninger, K. (1948). Changing concepts of disease. *Annals of Internal Medicine*, 29, 318–325.

———. (1959). The psychiatric diagnosis. *Bull Menninger Clinic*, 23, 226–240.

Morelli, D., & Koenigsberg, M. R. (1992). Sample medication dispensing in a residency practice. *Journal of Family Practice*, 34(1), 42–48.

Morone, J. A. (1993). The health care bureaucracy: Small changes, big consequences. *Journal of Health Politics, Policy and Law*, 18(3), 723–739.

Moscovici, S. (1993). The return of the unconscious. *Social Research*, 60(1), 39–93.

Nadelson, C. C. (1993). Ethics, empathy, and gender in health care. *American Journal of Psychiatry*, 150(9), 1309–1314.

Newman, F. (1991). *The myth of psychology*. New York: Castillo.

Newton, W., Goldstein, A., & Frey, J. (1992). There is no such thing as a free lunch. *Journal of Family Practice*, 34(1), 32–34.

Nietzsche, F. (1968). *Will to power*. New York: Random House.

———. (1972). *Ecce homo*. Munich: Goldmann Verlag.

Nussbaum, M. C. (1986). *The fragility of goodness: Luck and ethics in Greek tragedy and philosophy*. Cambridge, UK: Cambridge University Press.

Pardes, H. (1989). Educating psychiatrists for the 1990s. *Academic Psychiatry*, 13(1), 3–13.

Pardrutt, H. (1992). *Und sie bewegt sich doch nicht*. Zurich, Switzerland: Diogenes.

Pauleikhoff, B. (1983). *Das Menschenbild im Wandel der Zeit: Ideengeschichte der Psychiatrie und Psychologie*. Hürtgenwald, Germany: Guido Pressler Verlag.

Pincus, H. A., Henderson, B., Blackwood, D., & Dial, T. (1993). Trends in research in two general psychiatric journals in 1969–1990: Research on research. *American Journal of Psychiatry*, 15(1), 135–142.

Poling, A., Gadow, K. D., & Cleary, J. (1991). *Drug therapy for behavior disorders*. New York: Pergamon Press.

Prather, J., & Fiddell, L. S. (1975). Sex differences in the content and style of medical advertisements. *Social Science and Medicine*, 9, 613–618.

Prizzia, R., & Mokuah, N. (1991). Mental health services for native Hawaiians: The need for culturally relevant services. *Journal of Health and Human Resources Administration*, 14(1), 44–61.

Pryor, D. (1990). A prescription for high drug prices. *Health Affairs*, 9(3), 101–109.

Pucci, P. (1992). *Oedipus and the fabrication of the father*. Baltimore: Johns Hopkins University Press.

Ray, W. A., Griffin, M. R., & Shorr, R. I. (1990). Adverse drug reactions and the elderly. *Health Affairs*, 9(3), 114–122.

Richards, R. L., Kinney, D. K., Kunde, I., & Benet, M. (1988). Creativity in manic-depressives, cyclothymes, and their normal first-degree relatives: A preliminary report. *Journal of Abnormal Psychology*, 97, 281–288.

Rilke, R. M. (1977). *Lyrik und Prosa*. Käte Hamburger (Ed.). Frankfurt: Insel Verlag.

Robbins, S. L., Cotran, R. S., & Kumar, V. (1984). *Pathologic basis of disease*. Philadelphia: W. B. Saunders.

Rosin, U., & Köhler, G. K. (1991). Psychodynamic aspects of psychopharmacology in functional somatic complaints. *Psychotherapy and Psychosomatics*, 56(3), 129–134.

Roszak, T. (1992). *The voice of the earth*. New York: Simon & Schuster.

Rudnytsky, P. L. (1987). *Freud and Oedipus*. New York: Columbia University Press.

Sabshin, M. (1990). Turning points in American psychiatry. *American Journal of Psychiatry*, 147, 1267–1274.

Samuels, A. (1993). *The political psyche*. London: Routledge.

Scott, C. E. (1992). The pleasure of therapy. *ellipsis*, 2, 131–150.

Scull, A. T. (1979). *Museums of madness*. London: Penguin Books.

———. (1981). *Madhouses, mad-doctors and madmen: The social history of psychiatry in the Victorian Era*. Philadelphia: University of Pennsylvania Press.

———. (1988). *Desperate remedies: A social history of somatic treatments for mental illness*. Oxford, UK: Polity Press.

———. (1989). *Social order, mental order*. Berkeley: University of California Press.

Searle, J. R. (1993). The problem of consciousness. *Social Research*, 60(1), 1–16.

Shabahangi, N. R. (2003). *Faces of aging*. San Francisco: Elders Academy Press.

———. (2011). *Elders today: Opportunities of a lifetime*. San Francisco: Elders Academy Press.

————. (Ed.). (2011). *Gems of wisdom: A book of elder poetry and prose*. San Francisco: Elders Academy Press; Barnes & Noble.

————. (2012). *Encounters of the Real Kind: Musings, Stories, Poetry about Elders, Forgetfulness and Life* (Book 1). San Francisco: Elders Academy Press.

————. (2015). *Encounters of the Real Kind, Book II: Musings, Stories, Poetry about Elders, Forgetfulness and Life* (Book 11). San Francisco: Elders Academy Press.

Shabahangi, N. R., & Szymkiewicz, B. (2006). *Deeper into the soul*. San Francisco: Elders Academy Press.

Silver, A.-L. S. (1992). Intensive psychotherapy of psychosis in a decade of change. *Psychiatric Hospital*, 23(2), 49–54.

Skultans, V. (Ed.). (1975). *Madness and morals: Ideas on insanity in the nineteenth-century*. London: Routledge & Kegan Paul.

Sophocles. (1984). *The three Theban plays: Antigone, Oedipus the King, Oedipus at Colonus*. Robert Fagles (Trans). New York: Penguin Classics.

Spiegelberg, H. (1969). *The phenomenological movement: A historical introduction* (2 vols.). The Hague, Netherlands: Martinus Nijhoff.

Spitzer, M., & Maher, B. A. (Eds.). (1990). *Philosophy and psychopathology*. New York: Springer Verlag.

Stone, D. A. (1993). The struggle for the soul of health insurance. *Journal of Health Politics, Policy and Law*, 18(2), 287–317.

Strachey, J. (Ed. & Trans.). (1953–1974). *The standard edition of the complete psychological works of Sigmund Freud* (Vols. 1–24). London: Hogarth Press.

Strenger, C., & Omer, H. (1992). Pluralistic criteria for psychotherapy: An alternative to sectarianism, anarchy, and utopian integration. *American Journal of Psychotherapy*, 46(1), 111–130.

Streufert, S., & Gengo, F. M. (Eds.). (1993). *Effects of drugs on human functioning*. Zurich, Switzerland: Karger Verlag.

Sullivan, M., Verhulst, J., Russo, J., & Roy-Byrne, P. (1993). Psychotherapy vs. pharmacotherapy: Are psychiatrists polarized? — A survey of academic and clinical faculty. *American Journal of Psychotherapy*, 47(3), 411–423.

Swazey, J. (1974). *Chlorpromazine in psychiatry: A study of therapeutic innovation*. Cambridge, MA: MIT Press.

Talbott, J. A., Hales, R. E., & Yudofsky, S. C. (Eds.). (1988). *Textbook of psychiatry*. Washington, DC: American Psychiatric Press.

Thompson, K. S. (1993). Re-inventing progressive community psychiatry: The use of history. *Community Mental Health Journal*, 29(6), 495–507.

Toews, J. E. (1991). Historicizing psychoanalysis: Freud in his time and for our time. *Journal of Modern History*, 63(3), 504–545.

Toner, R. (1994, February 6). The family doctor is rarely in. *New York Times*, sec. 4, p. 1.

Trimble, M. R. (1988). *Biological psychiatry*. Chichester, UK: John Wiley & Sons.

Tuke, S. (1979). Description of the retreat (York, 1813). In A. T. Scull, *Museums of madness* (pp. 216–217). London: Penguin Books.

Verlust, J. (1991). The psychotherapy curriculum in the age of biological psychiatry. *Academic Psychiatry*, 15(3), 120–131.

Vernant, J. P., & Vidal-Naquet, P. (1990). *Myth and tragedy in ancient Greece*. New York: Zone Books.

Verwey, G. (1985). *Psychiatry in an anthropological and biomedical context: Philosophical presuppositions and implications of German psychiatry, 1820–1870*. Dordrecht, Netherlands: D. Reidel.

Voris, E., Shabahangi, N., & Fox, P. (2009). *Conversations with Ed: Why are we so afraid of Alzheimer's Disease?* San Francisco: Elders Academy Press.

Wallis, C., & Willwerth, J. (1992, July). Schizophrenia: A new drug brings patients back to life. *Time*, 53–58.

Wilkes, M. S., Doblin, B. H., & Shapiro, M. F. (1992). Pharmaceutical advertisements in leading medical journals: Experts' assessments. *Annals of Internal Medicine*, 116(11), 912–919.

Wiseman, R. (2003). *Therapies of literature: How long has it been since the future?* San Francisco: Elders Academy Press.

Working Group on Managed Competition. (1994). Managed competition: An analysis of consumer concerns. *International Journal of Health Services*, 24(1), 11–23.

Wyngaarden, J. B., & Smith, L. H. (Eds.). (1988). *Textbook of medicine*. Philadelphia: W. B. Saunders.

Wysowski, D. K., Schober, S. E., Wise, R. P., & Kopstein, A. (1993). Mortality attributed to misuse of psychoactive drugs, 1979–1988. *Public Health Reports, 108*(5), 565–570.

Yager, J. (1990). The many quests of psychiatrists: How well can we fulfill them? *Academic Psychiatry, 14*(1), 44–53.

Yalom, I. (1980). *Existential psychotherapy.* New York: Basic Books.

Yassa, R., Nastase, C., DuPont, D., & Thibeau, M. (1992). Tardive dyskinesia in elderly psychiatric patients: A 5-year study. *American Journal of Psychiatry, 149*(9), 1206–1211.